<u>Training Your Own Psychiatric Service Do</u>

MW01493877

Copyright © 2011 by Katie Gonzalez
Photography by Charlene Mendoza & Katie Gonzalez

Gonzalez, Katie.
ISBN 978-1-105-01787-2

Contents

Little Angels
Service Dogs

A psychiatric service dog can bring a dramatic change to the life of someone with a psychiatric disorder, but only if the dog is trained well enough to assist. A service dog is there to make your life easier, however a poorly trained dog will only make the situation more difficult.

This book will go over everything from the selection of the perfect dog, the details of training a dog in specific tasks that will assist you with your disability, to guidance in proper service dog etiquette for public access, and the laws involved with bringing a psychiatric service dog into public settings within the United States.

We are contacted by hundreds of people every year who are seeking certification for their dog to gain public access. Unfortunately in most of these cases it is clear that owners are trying to find a way to take their pet dogs with them into public, or to allow them access to pet-free housing. The truth is that most animal lovers would feel more comfortable bringing their pets with them to the grocery store – but this book is not for them. This book was written for those who suffer from life-inhibiting psychiatric disabilities, who would otherwise be unable to function without the help of a trained service dog.

A psychiatric service dog is not there only to provide emotional support. A true service dog is trained in specific tasks to assist their disabled handler. Then, and only then, is the animal permitted public access.

The material gone over in this book will teach real tasks that will make a difference in your disability.

The Americans with Disabilities Act defines a service animal as "a dog that is individually trained to do work or perform tasks for an individual with a disability. The task(s) performed by the dog must be directly related to the person's disability."

It is true that with many psychiatric disabilities the handler would be reassured simply by having the dog walking next to them, however there are

many other tasks a dog can be taught that will assist in great ways.

No one should try to find ways to take advantage of our rights. And no one should be 'looking' for new 'training tasks' simply so that it can accompany them into public.

This book will not waste your time. It is specifically meant for the disabled individual who has little to no experience with dog behavior or ownership, and will cover everything from basic obedience to advanced task training.

If you are an individual who also suffers from other disabilities, you will want to use this book in conjunction with our other books.

Is a Service Dog Right for You

What a waste of time it would be for you to go through all the trouble of selecting and training a service dog, only to find out that a service dog was not in your best interest to start with. This book will give you realistic expectations so you have the tools to determine if you should proceed.

Patience

First and foremost you must be patient. Even training obedience to a pet dog takes a great amount of patience, but a dog will require even more. It will take months before your dog is able to respond consistently to commands with the distractions of a public setting. But anyone who has patience can train a service dog.

Reactions of the General Public

The public in general is still somewhat naive about what constitutes a service dog. Many still believe that service dogs only come in the form of guide dogs and mobility assistance dogs. There are many disabilities that cannot be seen, such as psychiatric disabilities, seizures, and hearing impairments. I often tell people, "Most disabilities are invisible".

It is our job to educate the public on the various ways that dogs can assist with different disabilities, and great progress is being made, however, even long after your psychiatric service dog is trained, you will still have people assume that you are training the dog for someone else. You will hear many comments from the people around you. "See that dog, honey. That trainer is teaching the dog how to be a guide dog for the blind." Some will talk to you directly. "What great work you are doing, training this dog for the disabled!" Little do they know that the disabled party is actually you. These are all things that take getting used to, but most handlers use it as an opportunity to educate the public.

Feeling Comfortable in Public Settings

Many who suffer from psychiatric disabilities struggle going into public for various reasons. Some are more comfortable if they have a friend or family member accompanying them. Service dogs work well for these individuals because companionship helps them face the trials of the public setting. Others are not comfortable going into public even with the help of another person. If that scenario fits your situation it is likely that a dog will not make you feel comfortable either.

When you are in the socialization and training phases of training with your dog you will need to work on training in public locations. The reality is that training a dog in the public setting has its difficulties, even when the handler feels comfortable with the public watching so closely. You will have many eyes on you when working with your dog, people will be asking you questions about your dog because they are fascinated with service dogs, and at the same time your dog will likely be testing you by not responding to obedience commands. This only happens in the beginning phases, but you have to work through it before it gets better. For some this is manageable because they already feel more comfortable in public because of their dog's companionship (even though the dog is misbehaving). For others, the struggle of working with a disobedient dog in a setting that already makes them uncomfortable is too difficult.

Think on the past, to visits you have made into the public setting, and analyze how you dealt with the situation. Try to envision training a dog at the same time. Do you think it is the right choice to train your own psychiatric service dog? If not, you may want to seek outside help from a service dog trainer or assistance dog school.

Communication with the Public

Even after your dog is trained, you will receive more attention than you did without one. The public is interested in service dogs, and many will come over to talk to you about your dog simply because they are fascinated. Strangers will strike up conversations in checkout lines, and some will even stop you as you are making your way through the mall. Generally the public view of service dogs is a positive one, but you will receive questions out of their curiosity.

And I promise you will also hear many stories about all the dogs other people have had. It seems to be a rule that when someone sees a service dog they suddenly have the desire to share all their life experiences about every dog they've ever had.

I look at all of this as a positive. Your dog becomes a social bridge, opening up doors of communication that otherwise would be non-existent.

Time Constraints

Taking a service dog with you into public will add an average of 2 minutes to any outing. This is not a horrendous amount of time of course, but it does slow you down if you are in a hurry. Take into consideration that it will take a little more time getting in and out of your vehicle to make sure your dog is properly secured, and that you will be giving your dog the opportunity to relieve itself before entering any buildings.

Where Can You Go

A service dog is granted legal access to accompany you anywhere that the public is permitted; restaurants, shops, grocery stores, theaters, amusement parks, public transportation, etc.. The only exceptions to this are certain wards in a hospital, and certain animal related areas such as various sections of zoos. Certain airlines will have different criteria before allowing you to travel with your psychiatric service dog – such as a letter from your doctor – but travel with your service dog is not to come with any additional travel fees. In fact most airlines will even ship your dog's crate separately with the cargo for free. The Department of Transportation rules (14 CFR part 382) require airlines to allow passengers to fly with their service animals in the cabin on all U.S. Airlines, and they do not need to be confined to a crate or cage.

Some disabled handlers go as far as to assume that they are also legally allowed to bring their service dogs with them into privately owned residences. This is not the case. So when you are accepting an invitation to a friend's home for dinner, make sure to ask if you can bring your service dog along. It is the polite thing to do.

The law applies to all businesses open to the public. But business owners can't interrogate owners to assure the animal is a legitimate helper.

The law states:
In situations where it is not apparent that the dog is a service animal, a business may ask only two questions:

1)   Is the animal required because of a disability?

2)   What work or task has the animal been trained to perform?

No other inquires about an individual's disability or the dog are permitted. Businesses cannot require proof of certification or medical documentation as a condition for entry.

For information regarding travel in flight you can visit;
www.faa.gov/passengers/fly_pets/cabin_pets

For information regarding the Americans with Disabilities Act, and to check on current updates you can visit;
www.ada.gov

More laws and legalities will be discussed later.

Expenses, Grooming, and Maintenance
It is highly recommended to invest in a pet health insurance plan. You will want something in writing that states your service dog will be covered, and not only pet dogs. You will also want to make sure that your plan covers most medical situations. For example, a good policy would charge a small deductible of under $100.00, but cover 100% of additional medical expenses, regardless of the medical condition or procedure. You should expect to spend between $30.00-$40.00 per month for a pet health insurance plan.

Grooming is another expense you will want to consider. I strongly suggest learning how to groom your dog yourself. With some quality grooming supplies and training you should be able to handle this on your own without the additional expense of up to $100.00 a month for a professional. Keeping your service dog clean and odor free is essential to proper service dog etiquette. No one wants to be around an offensive dog.

A premium quality dog food will also be essential to your dog's health and longevity. You will want to feed a corn free diet. Most foods would come to an average of $40.00 a month for a larger breed of dog. Feeding a raw diet is more expensive, and requires a great deal of education and planning to get it right, but would be worth it in the end. Most high quality dog foods are not sold in grocery stores, but are reserved for sale in pet stores. Not all dog foods are available in all areas, so it would be best to ask your veterinarian what they would recommend.

Do I Need a Yard?

Absolutely not. Your service dog is your full time companion. He will accompany you almost everywhere you go. You will also be certain to give your dog the proper exercise – and proper exercise is not just a turn out into the back yard. Your service dog will be a much happier animal than the dog who lives outside on a 40 acre ranch. After all, how many dogs get to go out for a good day of department store shopping? That can be exhausting to even the most dedicated of shopping connoisseurs.

The Right Dog for Your Needs

If you already own a dog, or have a specific dog in mind, this will give you great insight as to if your dog is suitable for the type of work required of a psychiatric service dog. If you do not have a dog in mind yet, this will give you the tools needed to find your perfect match.

Dog Size

For most people with a psychiatric disability the size of the dog will not be a factor, but there are a couple points you should consider.

1) Do you need a dog large enough to help with other tasks. Many psychiatric medications can cause dizziness. A larger dog would also be able to help you with balance by wearing a specialized mobility harness to help stabilize you. Some people who suffer from other disabilities may also find it useful for a dog to retrieve items from off of the floor. A small dog would have trouble lifting heavy items, and would also have a hard time reaching high enough to put them in your hand or lap.

2) Would you feel more secure with a large dog by your side? A small dog may not offer the comfort of a more substantial dog.

3) Do you often take public transportation? Although most disabled handlers have large dogs and travel with them fairly easily, it would certainly be easier to tuck a Chihuahua in the aisle of a bus, than a Malamute.

4) Keep in mind that in general the public is still somewhat naive as to what constitutes a service dog. There are many, many individuals who have miniature breeds serving as assistance dogs, but they do receive more questions from the public, as compared to someone who has a yellow Labrador. This is of course a wonderful opportunity to educate others that any dog can be a service dog.

5) A large dog is easy for others to see in crowded situations. If you have a small dog you will have to make sure that others do not step on him, and you may end up carrying him or putting him in your lap.

6) While a large dog can be used as a deterrent, we will never want to train one specifically for protection. A dog who is trained to bite or be suspicious will be a liability in public. If you required assistance from a person, and your dog is protecting you, no one will be able to get near enough to help you.

7) If you are planning to let your small dog ride in grocery carts for the ease of shopping, think again. Your dog will have to walk on the floor, or ride in a bag that you carry. It is not proper service dog etiquette to allow a dog to be anywhere except for on the floor, or in your arms or lap.

Dog Breeds

Some dog breeds are easier to train than others. For example, a Basset Hound is more difficult to train than a Poodle. All dogs can be trained, but considering trainability may save you energy later.

If you have a separate disability and will be teaching the dog to retrieve, then you may want to select a breed that is a natural retriever.

If there is someone in your family who is allergic to dogs, you may want to select a poodle, or a poodle mix, such as a Labradoodle or Goldendoodle. Keep in mind that not all poodle mixes are hypoallergenic. The type of coat needs to be taken into consideration. Purebred Poodles, and Australian Labradoodles would be your best choice for allergies. Australian Labradoodles have been so tightly monitored for so long that we have a better guarantee of them having a hypoallergenic coat. There is not such a strong guarantee with an F1, F2 or F3 Labradoodle (first, second, or third generation).

In our school we usually use Labrador Retrievers, Golden Retrievers, and all sizes of Poodles. This is due to their friendly personality and easy trainability.

On occasion we will use German Shepherds, but only on a case-by-case basis. Many German Shepherds tend to be whiny, so selection is important. German Shepherds and other herding or guarding breeds are very watchful and are alert to almost everything that is going on around them. That is useful in some situations, and in others it is not. When deciding on a German Shepherd or similar guard or herding breed keep in mind that they are a naturally protective breed, and if your dog ever has it in his mind to 'protect' you in public, he will be a liability and cannot be used. That is not to say that you cannot raise and train some dogs away from these traits, but these protective instincts usually do not show themselves until the dog is 5 months old, or in an older dog who has finally become comfortable with his surroundings. And most dogs cannot be trained away from their natural instincts. Much of this has to do with genetics. I agree that bad dogs are made, not bred. However, a protective dog is not a bad dog, it is simply doing what it was genetically designed to do.

Mixed Breed or Purebred

If you are going to purchase a purebred dog you will need to do your research. Most purebred dogs come from breeders who put little to no care into their breeding programs. This creates dogs who suffer from genetic health problems, and/or temperament problems. When looking for a reputable breeder it is easiest to only consider dogs whose parents are OFA certified for good hips and elbows. This can be a costly certification for the breeder, so in most cases it is only done on dogs of excellent breeding and temperament. OFA certification shows that the breeder has put time and thought into the breeding. It also gives the puppy a higher chance of having good joints. These dogs will obviously cost more than dogs coming from a poor breeder, but it is well worth the investment. A dog with dysplasia will not make a good service dog as it causes them pain just to move around.

If you select a mixed breed dog there is the benefit of being able to rescue a dog from a shelter, and there is generally very little cost associated with the adoption. The down side to adopting a dog from the shelter is that you do not have any background information on the dog's lineage or health.

You can also adopt a purebred dog from a purebred rescue group. There are many organizations that specialize in rescuing specific breeds of dogs. In many of these cases the dogs are housed in foster homes where they receive individual attention in a home environment while they are awaiting their final adoption. In these cases the rescue often has background and health information on the dog, and can inform you of the behaviors they have witnessed the dog exhibiting.

When it comes down to it, you are much better off in using a mixed breed dog, than a poorly bred Purebred dog.

Gender

Males and females are both very similar in temperament as long as they are neutered. With a service dog you will definitely want to neuter as soon as your dog is old enough. It generally will make your dog calmer, and it takes away any chance of your dog developing uterine or testicular cancer, which is very common in older dogs. A female who is not spayed will bleed twice a year, and you won't be able to take her into public with you. A male who is not neutered will have a hard time paying attention to commands if there is a female in heat anywhere in the neighborhood.

Positives of Adopting an Adult Dog

1)An adult dog is easier to potty train because they have usually developed bowel and bladder control for longer periods of time.

2)Because of their maturity it is easier to train new tasks.

3)Adult dogs are generally calmer and not quite so hyperactive as a puppy.

4)Adult dogs are usually past their chewing phase. Your furniture has a great chance of survival. Retriever breeds may always want to put things in their mouths.

5)You get a guarantee of the size of your dog. As long as your dog is at least 1 year of age, it probably won't get any taller, although some dogs continue to bulk up until about 3 years of age.

6)With an adult dog of two years of age you can have x-rays of the joints sent in for an OFA reading. A dog younger than two years of age can still have a preliminary screening for healthy joints, but the joints are not done growing until two years of age. (Make sure your veterinarian knows the protocol for taking x-rays for an OFA reading).

If you are not taking x-rays you can watch the dog's gait as they trot and run. With an adult dog you should be able to see if there is a limp or any soreness when moving, although this does not rule out joint problems that will pop up in the future. An OFA reading is still recommended. Puppies are often too clumsy when moving to tell if they have even the slightest issue.

Negatives of Adopting an Adult Dog

1)It is hard to find an adult dog that has had a good amount of socialization. Usually any adult dog that is available is through a rescue or a private party who no longer wants the dog. Dogs who have had the right socialization as puppies usually don't find themselves in a rescue situation because they had dedicated owners to start with.

2)We have rescued many adult dogs through our school, and some have worked out beautifully. You can do this as well, as long as you are willing to look at a lot of different dogs. For every dog that we adopted, there were about 50 others we looked at that failed temperament testing. Also, out of the adult dogs that we have rescued, only half of them have graduated. The others simply didn't have the proper socialization before we adopted them. Even though they do well in initial temperament testing, it does not mean they are perfect. Many questionable behaviors, such as growling at men or chasing cats, take a while to show up.

3)Adult dogs often have bad habits, such as jumping up on people, or chasing cats. This book will explain how to deal with these problems, but it is still another factor to consider.

Positives of Adopting a Puppy

1)When adopting a puppy you are starting with a clean slate. You can avoid bad habits before they even start.

2)Because of your puppy's age it will be much easier to socialize. You can prevent any unwanted experiences, such as negative experiences with other dogs, or children.

Negatives of Adopting a Puppy

1)Most breeds will chew on as many things as they can put in their mouth as a puppy. This usually happens when they are teething, and has another quick visit at around 10 months of age. Retriever breeds may put things in their mouths throughout their entire lives.

2)You will need to work with your puppy to develop bowel and bladder muscles so they can go for longer periods of time without going potty. It usually takes longer to potty train a puppy than an adult dog.

3)Puppies are always more energetic, but keep in mind that many adult breeds are still rambunctious. Selecting a calm dog to start with is gone over later in this book in Temperament Testing.

4)Even if your puppy has come from parents who are OFA certified for healthy joints, it is still difficult to tell if your puppy has healthy joints until they can walk with more stability.

5)You should not run with a puppy until their joints are done growing, which is between 1-2 years of age, depending on the breed.

Temperament Testing a Puppy

When selecting a puppy from a litter, you will want to stand back and observe the puppies playing together. If possible, visit the puppies more than once so you can get a better idea of their temperament – you might be visiting on a day when a particular puppy is more sleepy than usual, or more rambunctious than usual.

You don't want the puppy in the corner that only observes what is going on around him. Nor do you want the puppy that initiates play or trouble. You want a puppy that is somewhere in the middle.

Drop a new tennis ball into the pen and see who comes to check it out. Make sure it is a new ball so you don't pass germs onto the puppies. You can roll it by the puppies and see who follows it. It is always better to select a dog with some amount of prey drive so you can play fetch with them later. Fetch is a very easy way to exercise a dog. If you will ever be using the dog to retrieve items for you as a task, then you definitely want a dog that chases the tennis ball. Keep in mind that very young puppies have poor eyesight, and may not be able to see the ball after it rolls too far away from them. This would be a test to conduct when the puppies are at least 7 weeks of age.

Next you can walk into the pen and get down on their level. Notice which ones come towards you, and which ones back away. You do not want one who backs away.

While you are down on their level make some noise with a wooden spoon against a pot or pan. Don't scare the puppies, but do make the noise sudden. It is okay if the puppies jump, but you want one who recovers quickly. You don't want the one who runs away or huddles in a corner. You don't want a reaction of fear or aggression.

If the puppies have not been exposed to being on their backs, it may not be a useful to roll the puppy over as a test. Many breeders interact with their puppies frequently and hold them on their backs often. Even a dominant puppy will do this well if he is exposed to it enough. A submissive puppy who has never been exposed to it may resist.

Ask the breeder which pup they think would be a good choice for what you need, and take it into consideration. Overall you should make the decision. If you have read this entire book, you will have a good idea of what to look for – a breeder may not.

If you are selecting a puppy from a breeder you will want to be sure that both parents (sire and dam) are available for you to greet. If only one is available you shouldn't even bother going to see the puppies. When you greet the sire and dam they may be excited to see you at first, but they should calm down after a few minutes. If not, the puppies may grow to be too hyperactive. Neither of the adult dogs should show any sign of fear or aggression. If they do, keep looking.

If you are selecting a puppy from a shelter it may be alone in its kennel. If it is you won't be able to compare it to the other pups. Walk into the kennel with the puppy and interact with it. If the puppy runs away from you or hides in the corner, keep looking. If the puppy is alone it may be starved for attention, so may jump and nip playfully at you when you enter. This is not necessarily a sign that the dog will be too much to handle. He may just be lonely and very excited to have company.

You will still want to make some sudden noises to see how he reacts. If you don't have anything else with you, toss your keys on the floor. Try to make noise with them and see how the puppy reacts. We just want to make sure that he recovers quickly. We don't want signs of fear or aggression.

Temperament Testing an Adult Dog

When selecting an adult dog, don't expect it to be well behaved. Remember that you will be the one doing the training. The dog may jump up on you, pull on the leash, etc. This book is here to help you fix all of that.

Overall, you are looking for a dog that is confident and unafraid. The dog should not be timid around strange objects, and should be very friendly to everyone and everything.

When temperament testing an adult dog at a shelter keep in mind that they may be displaying a different temperament in that environment than they would if they were calm and relaxed. The shelter can be very stressful for dogs. Although shelter staff generally try to make dogs comfortable, there is usually still a sense of unease and uncertainty.

You still want to make sure the dog does positively with the tests, but keep in mind that he may become more dominant or aggressive once he settles into your home. If that is the case, you will want to get another dog. A dog with aggressive tendencies cannot be used as a service dog for any reason. It is too great a risk to the publics' safety and your liability.

Only enter the kennels of adult dogs who are friendly. If you cannot tell from the outside of the kennel ask a staff member to assist you. When entering the kennel you will not reach down for the dog immediately. Let the dog come to you. It is okay if he jumps up on you while you are standing, but if you get down on his level and he is still jumping up, this is not the dog for you. You want him to show interest in you naturally, and you want him to come over for attention and to be pet. You do not want a dog that you have to coax over to you, or a dog who cowers in the corner. This is very important. Make sure he comes to you, without any bribery.

If he passes this first test ask if you can take him on a walk, or take him to a play area. Once out of his kennel he may pull and sniff around him. It may have been quite some time since he was out of his kennel, so keep this in mind. Once you are in the play area, you should be able to pull him over to you and pet him. He should at least want you to pet him for a moment before he gets distracted. If he cares nothing for you any longer, this may not be the dog for you. We want him to show some interest in you, even if there are other things for him to be doing – but don't expect him to ignore his sudden freedom of the kennel either.

When he is walking through the kennel aisles, make sure he is not showing aggression of any kind to other dogs. Make sure he is not cowering at tall objects, or shadows. Swing your hand above his head. Does he cower? If he does, does he recover quickly or does he look suspicious? Use what you can to make sudden or odd noises. See how he responds to them. Tarps, or suddenly opening umbrellas are a great tool.

Throw a tennis ball. Does he chase it? Try this a couple of times. If he at least picks it up at some point, this is good. We won't expect him to bring it back to you, or to carry it around in his mouth. He is probably too excited to be out of his kennel to pay too much attention to the ball.

He may be too stressed to eat treats, however if you get a dog that likes food you are way ahead of the game. Bring some hot dogs with you, and offer them. If he eats them up – wonderful! However, if he is stressed he won't want the food no matter what you do.

Remember that with adult dogs coming out of a shelter environment, that their temperaments may change once they are comfortably established in your home. If you see any aggression you cannot use the dog. He is now your responsibility, so make sure he gets a good home, but that home should not be yours. A professional trainer can help with his aggression problems, but he will then only be suitable as a pet. Not a service dog.

When adopting a dog that is in a foster home, or an individual's home, there is more you can do in the form of temperament testing. You can use treats to see if he is interested. When possible, we want a dog who is food motivated. He may not like biscuits, but see if he likes small pieces of hot dog. A dog who is not in a shelter should want the treats. If the dog does not want treats here when he is relaxed, keep looking. Having a dog that is food motivated will save you a lot of trouble later.

Explain what it is you are looking for in a dog, and ask if this particular dog fits the bill before you even drive out to see him. Then evaluate him yourself. In the end you are the one responsible for selecting your future partner.

If at all possible, bring a friend or family member with you – and if you are a woman, bring a man. If you are a man, bring a woman. We want to make sure the dog is not timid with either sex. Many dogs do well with women – fewer are confident around men.

Put on a baseball cap and sunglasses, and walk around slowly. You can even crouch a little on the ground. Try to look suspicious. How does the dog react? If it is fearful, move on.

Supplies

Now that you have selected your perfect partner you will need to make sure you have everything to take him home.

1) Leather Leash – 4 or 6 feet in length. Make sure to purchase a leash that is of quality leather. With the amount of time you will be holding your leash you will likely get calluses if using nylon.

2) Flat Collar – This can be made of nylon or leather. A flat collar is used mainly to display your dog's identification, and is not used for training very often. The flat collar does not cinch tighter, but always stays consistent. You want the collar to fit snugly on your dog's neck, giving space for 2 fingers between the collar and neck.

3) Head Halter – A head halter can be used on a dog that is older than 12 weeks. Do not actually use the halter until you have read the obedience section of this book. If you use a head halter incorrectly you can hurt your dog.

4) Chain Slip Collar – This is not to be used as a choke chain, although some retailers refer to them as choke chains because they cinch tighter. Do not use this on your dog until you have read the obedience section in this book. If used incorrectly you can seriously harm your dog. Only have your dog wear this collar while you are there to monitor because it has the ability to cinch tighter. Most dogs will benefit from training with a chain collar – very sensitive dogs, or dogs with a soft trachea should not use a chain collar. If your dog has trouble swallowing when you press your fingers against the underside of his throat, he may have a soft trachea. If you are uncertain make sure to ask your veterinarian. You will be visiting your veterinarian before any training.

5) Treats – Almost all dogs enjoy hot dogs. You can purchase healthy chicken or turkey hot dogs at your grocer. You can also use a treat called Pupperoni. I have found that dogs like these as well, and they are not as messy as hot dogs, but are more expensive. Biscuits are a waste of your money and are not good for training.

6) Dog Crate – You will NEED this for potty training. You want a crate that is big enough for your dog to stand up in and spread out, but not so big that he can go potty on one side, and get away from his mess on the other side. The type of crate you use is your choice. Most dogs will chew through a fabric crate. I prefer metal wire crates (which fold down nicely for storage, and have an open feel), or airline approved crates (which are mostly hard plastic). If your dog is a puppy and is growing, definitely get a wire crate with a divider. This way the crate can grow with your dog. More information on crates is in the potty training section.

7) Bowls – One for water, one for food. I highly prefer metal bowls, as bacteria can grow in the plastic bowls, which can actually give you dog acne or cause sickness or allergies. Getting a raised bowl that sits on a platform is desirable for larger breeds, but

not necessary. Make sure the water bowl is big enough to hold enough water so that you are not forced to refill it several times a day.

8) Toys – Unless you have a very small dog that doesn't like to chew, soft toys will be a waste of money. Most dogs will chew through stuffed toys in no time flat, which can be danger when your dog ingests the pieces. Every dog should have a Kong, or similar type of hard rubber or hard plastic toy that you can fill with treats and peanut butter. It will keep them active for hours and helps to exercise their jaws and clean their teeth. Hard nylabone products are also desirable as they are hard to destroy and offer the same chewing intensity as a Kong. Tennis balls are fun, but never leave them out. Dogs can tear off the outer coating of the tennis ball, then swallow the halves of the rubber inside, lodging it in their throat and cutting off air supply. Tennis balls are for monitored use only. Kong makes a chew-proof bouncing ball, slightly larger than a tennis ball that would be a good object to leave out, as long as your dog is not big enough to swallow it whole.

9) Rawhide – This is a good treat as long as your dog does not eat it right away. If they eat a lot it is just like leather sitting in their stomachs. Don't get rawhide that has large bulbs at the end, as these can get lodged in your dog's throat.

10) Shampoo – The best type of shampoo for dogs is made with oatmeal and conditions the coat nicely with all breeds. If you will be grooming your dog more than once every two weeks you should also use a conditioner.

11) Waste Bags – Also known as potty bags. Although it may be tempting to use a grocery bag instead, I have another use for these smaller bags. When you are out in public you can open up one of these little bags and fill it with water. With very little training your dog will learn to drink right out of the bag. This alleviates the need to carry around a separate collapsible bowl for your dog to drink out of. Just make sure your waste bags are unscented and powder free.

12) Ear Cleaner – There will be many brands available in the grooming section of your local pet store. Instructions are simple and listed on the bottle. You will also need cotton balls for your ear cleaner.

13) Squirt Bottle – This is used as a deterrent for your dog when teaching not to bark in the crate, etc..

14) Service Dog Vest – This is not a legal requirement, but it is recommended because it is easier for the public to recognize your dog as a working service dog. We purchase our vests in bulk from http://wolfpacks.com/products/servicedog, however you can purchase an individual vest from them as well. When selecting your patches, make sure to purchase an additional patch that labels your dog 'In Training". You can take this off later, instead of purchasing an entirely new vest.

I highly recommend getting a pocket in your vest so your dog can carry his own waste bags and identification. I will also recommend getting a vest with a ring to attach a leash.

15) Identification – After you have vaccinated your dog against rabies you will be provided with a rabies certificate from your veterinarian. You are then required to send that certificate to your local animal services department with an additional registration fee. In return they will send you a tag with a rabies license number engraved on it. This is something that is required of all dogs in almost every county. Some counties offer County Service Dog Licenses for service dogs in conjunction with rabies certification. This is just like your rabies license, but this will usually say Service Dog as well. Contact your county regarding their regulations. According to the ADA you are not required to have this extra service dog license. However every dog, even pet dogs, are required to have a rabies license that proves he has been vaccinated and registered in your county. This is the only legal tag you need, and it should be worn on your dog's flat collar at all times. A separate tag with your contact information should be on your dog's collar as well, for safety purposes, as the rabies license does not have your contact information engraved.

You can also purchase additional 'identification' online, but it is not necessary. Anyone can have 'identification' printed for their service dog.

We also give our recipients disposable cards to pass out that display the ADA laws and FAA regulations. This is useful if you have anyone question your rights to bring your dog into public. You can simply hand them one of these cards and walk away, without needing to explain.

The cards explain to contact the Department of Justice if they have any further questions. You can cards like this yourself, or you can purchase these cards from our website. www.littleangelsservicedogs.org

16) Nylon Leash – This leash is for use in the car and around the house. It should be thin and short. It's purpose is for consistency in training, and not for use on trips into public.

17) Long Line – This is a 15-30 foot leash used for training. They are generally inexpensive, and can be made of almost any material.

First Day Home

Now that you have your supplies it is time to take your dog home. Having your dog travel in a crate is the safest mode of transportation, but is very difficult when traveling with your dog so often, which you certainly will be. If this is a young puppy who has not been leash trained you will need to use a crate. However, if your dog is an adult the next best option is to use your Nylon Leash, as described in #16 of the previous chapter. Tie this leash to the non-retractable portion of the seat belt in the back seat of your car. Most cars have a fabric loop of the seatbelt attached to the clip. You will slip the nylon leash through that fabric loop. When you attach the leash to your dog's vest or collar you will only want enough leash so that your dog can barely sit up straight. This does not allow for a lot of slack in the leash. This is to prevent a lot of momentum gaining if you were in an accident, and will be less likely to injure your dog. Attaching the leash to the vest is obviously safer. You will want to make sure the vest is on your dog securely enough that he cannot wiggle out of it while you are driving.

Your number one priority when behind the wheel of a car is to pay attention to the road – not to pay attention to what your dog is doing in the back seat.

If you will be taking public transportation you will want your dog to sit or lay down between your legs, at your feet. Before he is trained to stay there, you may need to hold him there. This may prove to be a challenge in the beginning, but be consistent and he will learn to relax and just enjoy the ride.

Once you are home take care to introduce your dog to his new surroundings. Before entering the house let him explore any yard that is in front of the house so he can relieve himself if he needs to. Refer to the next chapter for proper potty training.

Introducing Other Pets

If you have any other pets, do not introduce them right away. Do what you can to keep them separated for the first day or two and allow them to grow accustomed to the other animal's scent. When you are ready put your dog in the crate and allow your dog to watch or greet the other animals through the gate of the crate. If your dog barks or jumps at the animals, use a squirt bottle and immediately spray your dog on the muzzle and say 'no' in a firm voice. Don't spray him in the nose or eyes, but be aware that he won't like his face being squirted and will quickly learn to avoid the behavior he used to cause the reaction from you. Stay consistent.

Eventually your dog will learn to be calm around these other animals. Once he shows some restraint inside the crate you can make introductions, but make sure that all dogs are on a leash. Be very careful in case someone reacts adversely. You should never leave your dog alone with the other animals until you are positive there will not be any problems – but never trust your dog with rodents or birds. This may be a period of weeks or months, never wait for just a period of a few days. If anything is predictable about animals, it is that they are unpredictable.

Potty Training

The first thing you will need to work on with your dog is potty training. Potty training a service dog is a lot different than house training a pet. This dog will be accompanying you into many different locations and he has to be potty trained in every one. Look at it from a dog's point of view; some of the stores you will enter have very tall ceilings with wide-open spaces. The lighting is usually very bright. Your dog may not realize you are indoors at all, but he still has to know that you are in control of when he relieves himself. He cannot squat in the middle of the cereal aisle.

Before you take your dog into public we will be working on potty training in your home. With all training, you need to take your time and be consistent.

Crate. Crate. Crate. No, it is not a cage. We want your dog to associate this as her den. Make sure the crate is NEVER in the sun, even for a minute. Put her toys inside. This is where you put your dog when you cannot watch her. Feeding her in the crate will also help her to associate this space as a den.

The idea of the crate is that a dog does not want to go potty in their 'den' and then have to sit in their excrement. If you have a puppy that will be growing, you should get a crate with a divider that can gradually move back in the crate slowly allowing more room for your puppy every couple of weeks. When using a divider in your crate make it just big enough that your puppy can stretch out and turn around comfortably. By doing this your puppy does not have enough room to potty on one side, and get away from the mess on the other. Your puppy will do her best to hold her bowels and bladder until you let her out.

With an adult dog you want the crate just the same size as you would for the puppy – just big enough to stretch out, but no larger.

If your dog is having accidents in the crate remove all bedding. Sometimes the absorbency makes it tolerable for them to go potty in there when they should be learning to hold it.

When your puppy is very young you can try 4 hours at the longest, and gradually go up to no more than 8-9 hours.

Every time you take her out of the crate, immediately take her outside to potty, while on leash.

ALWAYS be with your dog when she is going potty. THIS IS THE HARDEST PART OF RAISING A SERVICE DOG. SERVICE DOGS CAN ONLY GO POTTY WHEN THEY ARE TOLD. THEY NEED TO POTTY IN DIFFERENT AREAS, AND LEARN TO GO ON COMMAND. If you are walking your dog through the grass and she stops to potty, this is not okay – you should tug on the leash in tiny pops until she stops. Even though she is going outside, she is still not going when she was told. This is important because service dogs work in a variety of areas that may seem appropriate to relieve themselves in – but in reality it may be very inappropriate. They need to learn to hold it, until they are told.

As soon as you take the dog out of the crate, take her outside on leash – **in a new spot each time**. This last bit is also different than how you would train a pet dog. With pets it is best to have them potty in the same spot of the yard – with service dogs though, they need to learn to feel comfortable going on a variety of surfaces, with a variety of different smells, whenever they are commanded.

Stand there with your dog quietly while holding the leash. Do not let her know you are watching (do not make eye contact, she'll just stare back at you instead of sniffing the ground to go potty). Once your dog squats, very quietly start repeating 'go potty, go potty, go potty'. Eventually your puppy will associate 'go potty' as a need to relieve herself, and that's all you will have to say in the future in order to make her go.

Do you remember the Pavlov dog that salivated when he heard the bell? This was because the food and the bell were presented over and over again at the same time. The dog came to associate one stimulus with another – the bell with the food. Then later, when only the bell was presented, the dog still salivated.

This goes the same for presenting the stimulus of 'go potty, go potty, go potty' only when your dog is presented with the stimulus of actually relieving herself. Later she will hear 'go potty' and will automatically need to go. She isn't necessarily thinking that you want her to go – she just has the sudden urge to. This is called training through association.

As stated earlier, whatever goes in at a certain time will come out at a certain time. If she normally defecates at 9AM, wait until she defecates before letting her back in the house to romp around. If she does not defecate, and she usually does – or if she usually urinates, and has not – take her right back inside to the crate and give her more time, then repeat the process.

Once you are sure that your dog has nothing else in her system, it is safe to let her romp around the house WITH YOU. Don't leave your dog unattended. That is what the crate is for.

After your dog is trained she can stay out of the crate – for now, it is your lifeline.

Your dog now has a safe window of time, of about 15 minutes, depending on the dog, and how much they have had to eat and drink lately. When your time window is growing to an end, it is time to cuddle your dog for a while. Most puppies will not potty if they are being held in arms or on a lap, and most adult dogs will not go potty if they are forced to sit or lay down with you on the floor – if they are trying to get up though, it may be because they have to potty.

When you are done with cuddle time, it is back to crate time for a doggy nap – and possibly a doggy temper tantrum. If that is the case, do NOT give in and let your dog out. Not even once. If you do, you are just training your dog to cry in the crate to get out. If your dog is being relentlessly whiny, use the squirt bottle, set on a thin stream, and squirt her on the muzzle and say 'no – quiet'. You may need to do this several times, or several hundred times – but it will work eventually, depending on how diligent your puppy is. Just remain consistent.

If you turn your back, and your dog starts in again, immediately do the same thing again – they will get the idea. The whining only lasts for a couple of days this way, as long as you are consistent. I've known some of our puppy raisers who have slept with a squirt bottle in their hand, with the crate next to their bed. It works!

If you follow this sequence, your dog will never have an accident. Yes, it is possible. Many dogs have been house trained in just a couple weeks, and it is all because their handlers are consistent and don't allow room for mistakes. The more mistakes your dog has, the longer it will take for her to get in the habit of only going potty outside.

<u>Potty Training Sequence</u>

CRATE
POTTY
FREE TIME
CUDDLES
CRATE
REPEAT

When you take your dog out into public you will be following a similar structure. NEVER enter inside a building unless your dog has JUST gone potty right outside in the parking lot. I cannot be more adamant about this subject. The only handlers who have had accidents with their dogs inside of buildings did not wait for the dog to go potty outside. This usually happens because the handler is on a time schedule – and they have to get in and out of the store. My suggestion is simple – don't take your dog with you in the beginning if you are on a time schedule. Only take your dog with you when you have the time to wait, and wait, and wait some more.

When you first arrive at your destination and you exit the vehicle, you immediately take your dog over to a planter or landscaped area in the parking lot and tell them to 'go potty'. In the beginning they are usually too distracted to do anything but sniff and watch people walk by. If this is the case continue to be patient.

If it has been 15 minutes, take a walk around the block and work on training – or take a quick step inside the door of the establishment, and make an immediate u-turn and go right back out. Don't even stay inside the building for more than 5 seconds. This is just to get your dog over the initial intrigue of being in a new location. Sometimes the environmental changes will stimulate the dog to go.

Once your dog has gone potty, it is safe to bring him in the building. But if he has had a lot to drink he may have to relieve himself in 20 minutes, which means you give yourself 15 minutes of safe time.

While you are in a building always keep your dog in motion, unless he is in a down stay. If someone wants to talk to you, stop and immediately have your dog down. Your dog is never sitting, or standing still – always in motion, or in a down stay. This is the best way to keep your dog from going potty in a new building because dogs generally will not potty if they are walking or laying down.

This is a hard habit to get into initially, but it is the best tip of public access that I can offer you.

Chewing

All puppies chew. And unfortunately many adult dogs chew throughout their lives, and some will chew simply to let off stress, or because they are bored. However, this is controllable.

Don't allow your dog to roam unattended. This can be dangerous (electrical cords, poisons, your bossy cat). This is also dangerous for your furniture, clothing, shoes, rugs, remotes – basically anything and everything (even the children's toes). This is what the nylon leash is for. The leash is there so that you can give your dog a quick snap on the leash whenever he starts chewing on something other than his toy. If your dog starts chewing on a loose piece of paper, or an old shoe that you don't care about – take it away anyway! Your dog must learn that he can ONLY chew on his toys.

Some trainers say to have as many toys around as possible. This works for some dogs – but for others it only confuses them. Some dogs need 2-3 toys that all look and feel the same. That way it is very obvious to them what they can and cannot chew on. When there is a lot of variety in toys with different smells and textures, it can be hard to distinguish them from the shoes.

If you will be teaching your dog to retrieve items for you, it is desirable for your dog to pick up random items and bring them to you. So, instead of reprimanding your dog for putting something in his mouth, simply call him over and exchange whatever he has for the treat you offer him. If however he brings you something, without you calling him over, just take it – no treat. Otherwise he will start bringing you anything he can find to get that treat.

Health

The most important factor in your dog's health will be establishing a good relationship with your veterinarian. If you do not already have a veterinarian the best way to find one would be to contact your nearest emergency clinic. These clinics are open 24 hours a day and the doctors there were hired specifically because they are very good at what they do. These clinics often specialize in critical cases and don't regularly handle routine veterinary care. Because of this they can refer you to a good veterinarian to assist you with day-to-day needs.

Once you locate the veterinarian, schedule an appointment and take your dog in for an exam and consultation. If you have a puppy that is not done with its vaccines you will want to carry your dog the entire time. If you do put the puppy down on the exam table, or on the weight scale, ask the technician to disinfect the surface right then and there. Watch them do it. Remember, you are in an area that sick dogs have been. A good veterinary clinic is cleaned regularly, but puppies with parvovirus have been in contact with most of the surfaces.

In your exam ask your doctor to put your dog on a vaccination schedule and to recommend routine parasite control for both internal and external parasites. Most puppies are born with worms, but these are easily taken care of with medication.

Also make certain to get your dog on a heartworm treatment plan as soon as possible. This generally requires a blood panel for the prescription, but it is well worth it. Most states outside of Nevada, Arizona, and southern California carry a high potential for dogs to be infected with heartworm.

Make certain to tell your doctor that his newest patient is to be a service dog so that there is a clear understanding of the dog's health being of utmost importance. Your dog will be going into many locations that most pets do not go, and will be more active than most dogs. Also speak to your vet about your dog's joints, and go over any suggestions they have regarding proper care based on your dog's age and breed.

Grooming

Most grooming can be done by yourself. Not only will it help financially, but it can also be therapeutic.

Service dogs should be brushed daily even if they don't have a coat that sheds or tangles. Cleanliness is an important aspect when taking a dog into the public setting.

Consult with your veterinarian on how often you can bathe your dog without drying out the coat and skin. You will not want an offensive dog odor when walking your dog through a grocery store or restaurant.

Your doctor should show you how to clean your dog's ears. Some breeds are more prone to ear infections and will need a good ear cleaning every week, and possibly more often if they are in the water regularly.

You will also want to be shown how to trim your dog's nails without cutting below the quick, and how to brush your dog's teeth. In the beginning of a dog's life it may not seem necessary to brush their teeth, but as they get older this is the best way to avoid bad doggie breath.

There are certain grooming areas that should be addressed by a professional. Most dogs will need their anal glands expressed every six months. It is not necessarily a pleasant experience as I'm sure you can imagine. Some breeds could also use a good trim or shave every now and then, and this is difficult to execute well without a lot of experience.

When grooming your dog at home it is always best to secure your dog with a leash so you don't have to worry about him jumping out of the tub or shower while you are in the middle of soaping him up. If you do not have a safety rail or handle in your tub or shower you can purchase a 'suction tub & shower bar' from North Coast Medical by visiting www.ncmedical.com. These bars easily attach to your shower wall with suction cups. You can then tie your dog's leash to the bar, only allowing him 1 foot or less of leash between his collar and the bar. This will hold him securely still so you can bathe him with ease. Make sure to attach the leash to a flat collar (one that does not cinch tighter) in case he puts constant pressure on the leash – we don't want him to choke himself if he truly dislikes the water.

Another worthwhile investment is a hand-held shower head if you do not already have one. Make sure to test the water's temperature on your wrist before wetting your dog.

There are many dog shampoos available on the market, but please make sure to only use a tear free formula when washing your dog's face. Another good precaution is to avoid getting the insides of the ears wet; in fact it would be best to hold your dog's ear down against his head when running the water over his head and neck.

Most dogs are frightened of the hair dryer initially. Again, make sure he is on leash, outside of the tub, before you attempt to blow dry him. Hold him still, not allowing him to dart away, and turn the hair dryer on, pointing it away from him. Just allow him to become accustomed to the sound first. Once he relaxes with the sound, point the dryer slowly on his back legs, then only move up once he has relaxed to the feeling of the air towards the back of his body – he will be more concerned about the air hitting him around his head and ears.

Blow drying needs to be done with care – it would be easy to point the dryer in one place for too long and to burn your dog – make sure to move the dryer as much as possible, always feeling the coat to make sure he is not overheating.

Overtime your dog may even learn to love the hair dryer, and will come running whenever he hears you drying your own hair. My dogs all come running every morning. I give them each a few moments of hot-air-bliss before continuing with my own styling.

Important Note on Exercise

Please do not to overexert your puppy's joints too early, otherwise you can cause environmentally induced joint problems, known as dysplasia. Even though your puppy may have genetically sound joints, too much exercise can cause problems. Do not run, play fetch for more than 5 minutes at a time, or take your puppy on long walks. This should not be done with any dog that is under 2 years of age. Going up and down stairs, allowing your puppy to jump down out of a car instead of lifting, or excessive swimming can also cause the joints to grow abnormally.

It is of vital importance that service dogs have sound joints and good health. Otherwise their working career is greatly hindered.

Nutrition

Try to feed your dog whatever he is accustomed to eating for at least the first few days, then you can start gradually changing the food. Do so very slowly, with only 10% being the new food, and 90% the old. Continue daily like this until he is eating the new food. You never want to change a dog's diet abruptly as it can make them ill.

You will want to feed your dog a dry kibble that is grain free. Raw diets are wonderful if you can get them right, but it is very difficult to make sure your dog is getting all the nutrition he needs. It is far safer to stick with a dry kibble of a premium quality. Don't bother adding any wet food in with the dry. All this does is spoils your dog so that when you don't have the wet food, he won't eat it. Dry kibble is also excellent exercise for his jaws, and it is also good for his teeth.

The feeding amounts for adult dogs and puppies will be listed on the bag. In some cases the amount is based on the caloric intake needed in colder climates. If you see that your dog is not a healthy weight, it is time to feed less. You should be able to feel your dog's ribs, but not see them. And, just like people, they should have an obvious waist line.

There is no need to add any supplements to your dog's food unless your veterinarian recommends them. The premium dry kibble has everything your dog will need.

Make sure not to free feed your dog. Only offer food to an adult dog once or twice per day. A puppy should be offered food 3-4 times per day, depending on the age and breed. Very small breeds may need to be free fed as puppies, as their stomachs cannot hold very much as once – but as the small dog turns into an adult, it is time to pick up the food.

When feeding a large breed adult dog it is best to elevate the bowl, or to put a large obstacle in the food bowl so your dog needs to eat around it. Make sure the obstacle is far too big for your dog to put in his mouth. This will help prevent bloat – a deadly problem with dogs that occurs when they swallow too much air and their stomachs flip over. If you ever see your dog having trouble getting comfortable, and is trying to vomit, but can't – it is time to go to the vet, and time to get there quick.

We prefer to feed our dogs once a day in the evenings. This is because it leaves them hungrier for treats during the day while we are doing training. They get plenty of these treats during the day, but they are more motivated than if they ate a large breakfast.

It is also important to consider the fact that dogs, being carnivores, were meant to hunt their food and go for days without having a meal. Because of this their digestive system is designed very differently from ours. So don't feel bad for feeding your dog once per day. Many breeds are excellent at looking hungry all day long. Some dogs will eat themselves sick when given the opportunity.

It is best to feed your dog in her crate as it will help her to associate it as her den. Dogs in the wild often bring back their findings to their den. But still be sure to play with her food so she does not become possessive. Don't tease her with taking it away – just put your hand in there while she is eating.

However, if you have an adult dog that may already be possessive of food, this can be dangerous. You may want to try with the handle of a broomstick at first so you are further away if she snaps. You won't want to tolerate the snapping, and will want to tug on her leash as a correction. Make sure to tug the leash away from your body, and not towards it. Tugging away will also keep her from snapping at you.

Your last feeding of the day should be around 10 hours before you will take him out to potty in the morning. If you feed your puppy at 10PM, your puppy will need to defecate after he eats dinner, but then defecate again at around 8AM (10 hours later).

Always feed at the same time. Whatever goes in at a certain time, is going to come out at a certain time – and trust me, you want to know when your dog may need to potty.

Keep your dog's water bowl right outside the door that you use to take her out to potty. This way she is encouraged to go outside for two reasons; water and potty time. This way you can monitor how much your dog is drinking. Inside, your puppy may just start to play in it and make a big slippery mess on the floor. It is not necessary to have water available to your puppy at ALL times. It is however necessary to give your dog water frequently. In the beginning this is going to be around seven times per day. On days when you will be taking your dog into public, limit water in the mornings. But when you get home make sure to offer all the water they want.

Socialization and Training

Socializing a service dog properly can be tricky, especially if the dog is not yet done with vaccines. Socializing a puppy is important to do when they are young, but if they are not done with their vaccines you need to be very careful not to let them touch any surfaces where other dogs have been. This may mean carrying them with you everywhere you go. Initially this is a good idea anyway because they are not fully potty trained at such an early age, and carrying them will keep them from going potty in inappropriate areas.

When your dog is done with its vaccines you can start allowing your dog to walk where other dogs have been. A wonderful place to socialize a service dog in training is a large pet store. Most large pet store chains encourage owners to bring their dogs with them, which allows us even more opportunity for socialization due to all of the distractions. Some chains also have elevators, public restrooms, and stairs.

Socializing with People

When the dog is very young we can allow people to pet them, but as they get older this should stop. In fact, many service dogs will have a patch on the vest that says 'Do Not Pet Me, I'm Working'. The reason for this is that many dogs get so excited about the possibility of getting to meet someone new, that they stop paying attention to their handler and all control is lost. There are a few dogs who do not care one way or another if someone pets them, but this is usually not the case.

When the dog is young, we want them to learn that people are friendly, so interaction with friendly people is encouraged. You can ask strangers to give your puppy a treat or pet your puppy – they will gladly assist as most people have a hard time resisting a puppy in the first place.

When introducing children to your puppy you must make certain the children will be kind. No ear pulling, pinching, chasing, hitting or kicking. Only gentle petting. If dogs are exposed to anything that is frightening to them, they may even become aggressive towards children and then cannot be a service dog used for public access.

If you are planning to take your puppy on a walk through an elementary school you must be cautious, and maybe even have another person with you to keep the children from swarming all over the puppy. The children are just excited to see something so cute, but the puppy is wondering why they are running over, suddenly hovering, and reaching out. Having one child pet at a time would be good, but no more than that initially.

Introduce your dog to as many men as possible. This is sometimes harder to do because men are less likely to approach you in public to pet your dog, where you will get many women and children showing interest. Dogs view men differently than women

or children. Men naturally carry themselves differently than women do. Men generally have broader shoulders and exude more outward confidence, which to a dog looks domineering. Men will walk straight up to a dog, face it head on without the slightest angle to their bodies, and speak in a naturally lower voice. To dogs this is also domineering. A low voice is closer to a growl. Facing a dog head on without an angle to the body is exuding dominant body language. Men do this naturally. Women tend to carry themselves differently, with a slight flow to their step, and arms positioned in a way that appears welcoming. Women have higher voices, which to a dog sounds more inviting and less intimidating. The sweetest men in the world still have these traits whether they want to or not. This is very stereotypical of course, but men generally walk into a room like they own the place, and women as if they are visiting. This is not the case all the time, but for the most part this is natural. Dogs pick up on it. This is why many dogs are only afraid of men, even if they were raised by one. For your dog to only meet male family members is not enough, in fact they need to meet more men than women and children.

When your puppy seems to be friendly towards all people, men, women and children, it is time to stop allowing anyone to pet your dog. If you do not, your dog will be very hard to control in public settings.

Many handlers ask me what to say to people when they are reaching down to pet the dog. The handler does not want to sound mean or confrontational, but they know they cannot allow everyone to pet their dog for training purposes. So, this is exactly what you tell them. "I'm so sorry, my dog can't say hi. He's in training." Most people will apologize and say they didn't realize. You can continue on the subject if you wish by saying, "He is very friendly and loves saying hi to people – but that is the problem. If I let him say hi he will stop paying attention to me, and will be looking to everyone else for attention."

Socializing with Dogs

All of the socialization your dog needed with other dogs has already occurred. Your puppy's mother and siblings taught the social hierarchy. To dogs, everything is about hierarchy. Yes, most dogs like to play with other dogs, but hierarchy is being established even in play.

The 'do not say hi' rule applies to other dogs as well. How many times have you seen other pet dogs pulling on leash trying to reach another dog? It happens all the time because the owners allow them to say hello some of the time. The dog is left thinking that there is a chance, however small, and that they should try their very hardest to go greet the other dog. Again, this leaves us with a dog that is not paying attention to the handler.

Do not let your dog greet other dogs when working. That is any time your dog is in a command, such as heel, sit, down or stay, etc.. A working dog is not working only when he is wearing his service dog vest – he is working whenever you tell him to, which is when you give a command.

If you would like to set up play dates for your dog, feel free. But make sure the other dogs are friendly. Socialization NEEDS to be positive. If it is not, you are not doing your dog any favors by socializing him. If he thinks that dogs are mean, he will likely become aggressive towards them, and then he cannot be a service dog with public access. **With socialization we are basically tricking the dog into thinking that the world is a friendly place.** We have to protect our service dogs from anything that would bring them harm, mentally or physically. One good mauling from an aggressive dog could haunt your dog for life, and give you reoccurring problems with behavior.

In a play session dogs may snap at each other or even get in brief rolls, growls and teeth included – but it should not last for very long. This is the dogs working out their natural hierarchy – not to do so would be unnatural. But dogs who were poorly socialized (likely attacked by an aggressive dog in the past) will be aggressive towards your dog and cause the horrible cycle to start all over again.

You want to get your dog around other dogs very often. Take them on walks through large pet stores, parks, etc. and make sure your dog sees the other dogs, but knows they are not going to approach him or hurt him. He will learn to ignore them over time. Redirect your dog's attention back on you through training or a treat and praise him for looking at you even though there is another dog nearby.

If a stranger approaches you with their dog on leash, swerve away from them and they will usually get the drift that you are trying to avoid a meeting of your dogs. You can smile and be diplomatic about it and they won't be offended in the least. If they do not pick up on your signals, simply say 'Oh, my dog cannot say hi right now. He is a working service dog". They will apologize and move on.

Many owners think their dogs are friendly, when in fact they are not. Many dogs are only aggressive on leash. This is called leash aggression and occurs because the dog feels cornered and trapped not being able to get away.

In the end, your dog will be much better off avoiding other dogs, unless you are positive they are friendly, and your dog is not working at the time of the greeting.

Socializing to Strange Objects

Once your dog is doing well with following their commands in a pet store, start taking them to as many other places as possible. Take them to amusement parks where they can greet large costume characters, see an air show with jets flying over head, or take them to the theater where they can see the screen come to life in front of them. If your dog is afraid hold him still and comfort him.

There are three responses to fear; fight, flight or freeze. If the dog tries the 'flight' they will try to take off or run away. The more a dog moves away from an object, the worse they make it for themselves. Overreacting by darting away increases adrenalin and makes the situation worse. If the dog is held still and cannot dart or hide, they will acclimate and adjust. You can stroke under their chin and talk in a soothing voice. You can also try counter conditioning, which is where you try to turn a negative situation into a positive one. If the dog is afraid of the cars driving by on the street, offer a treat right as the car is driving by. This can get your dog to focus on you and the treat, and turns the noise of that car into something positive.

At times dogs are too nervous to eat in these situations, so they need to be introduced to the stimulus repeatedly. In the example for a fear of cars just get out a lawn chair and sit by the street, holding your dog securely by your side – over time they may get to the point where they are not so nervous, and may take that offered treat, then you can start counter conditioning.

Let's take costume characters as an example. It is not normal for your dog to witness a 10-foot penguin. When introducing your dog to something like this, do not have the costume character pet your dog. Just ask them to move as natural as possible. If the costume character stands very still it may actually unnerve your dog more. Dogs challenge each other by standing stiff and erect, so when they see others doing this it is a threat. The costume character can stand slightly sideways, not facing the dog directly, and just waddle back and forth. Later, once your dog is feeling safe, they can reach down to pet the dog, or maybe even hand your dog a treat. This is easier than you may expect, as most people (even the ones inside the costumes) are fascinated by service dogs and are very willing to help.

If your dog barks at anything that makes them nervous you will want to tug on the leash to correct them. This is cause and effect; the dog learns that if they bark, a negative occurs. The only negative involved with socialization is when the dog acts aggressively. This is not necessarily something to be concerned about in the beginning – they are barking because they are bothered but with proper socialization they won't be bothered anymore. Now, if your dog is barking in a threatening way, lunging or showing teeth, you can be concerned; this shows us that the dog's natural reaction to threats is to be threatening back – that is a potential safety issue. But a dog who merely barks because they are alert or afraid isn't something to be concerned about right away. We still want to correct it because a service dog should not bark in public, and we don't want the problem to get worse. If a dog is allowed to bark as an alert, they may later grow on that behavior and become aggressive.

Dogs can be taught to be more and more aggressive, which is clearly something we will not do with service dogs. As an example, there may be a dog that is nervous about a child that is staring at them, so the dog barks quietly – the child is unnerved by this and so backs away. The dog learned that by barking the threat left. The next time they bark quietly but the threat does not leave, so they bark louder and lunge, and that made the threat go away. That quickly turns into full out aggression. If that dog were corrected for barking, it would not have turned into aggression, and they could be socialized through it and learn to love children.

Amusement Parks

If your dog is extremely confident you can take him on certain rides at amusement parks. Some dogs do well with the Pirates of the Caribbean ride at Disneyland. This ride does not have sudden turns where the dog could be injured, but it does go down several slopes very quickly. If you think this could panic your dog, don't even try it. There are just some things that are too extreme for certain dogs. Most amusement parks will allow you into rides through the disabled entrance. This is to allow one person to stay with the dog while the rest of your party goes on the ride. When they are done riding, someone in your party can hold your dog while you go. Parks are very accommodating about this. Some parks even have a special Service Dog Waiting Area where you can put your dog in a crate that the park provides, and they have a park attendant stay with your dog while you go on the ride. This gives your dog a moment to take a much-needed nap. You would still go through the disabled entrance for this option and ask if they have a Service Dog Waiting Area.

Disneyland is very accommodating to service dogs, but as of 2011 they do not have Service Dog Waiting Areas with provided crates due to liability concerns. Sea World and Universal Studios provide several rides with Waiting Areas. Most zoos will provide you with an attendant to accompany you throughout the park, and may restrict your dog from certain areas due to animal related health and behavioral concerns.

Many amusement parks offer animal-related shows, where live animals perform on stage. Even though you may be asked to sit in the disabled seating area near the front, still request to sit in the back. You want your dog out of sight from the other animals.

When I first started training service dogs I brought a dog to one of these shows and sat in the front where I was asked to sit. My dog was the star of the show; the other animals focused on my dog throughout the 'performance' and refused to respond to their training due to their distraction. The dog I was training found the show entertaining, but at certain points I was concerned for his safety as many of the undomesticated , yet trained, animals tried to approach him.

In the end, use common sense when socializing your dog. Do not introduce your dog to situations unless he is ready for them, and never put your dog in a dangerous situation.

Obedience Training

The best way for most dogs to learn obedience training initially is through positive reinforcement alone. With this method dogs are initially lured into certain positions, and then rewarded with something they love. This teaches them what is wanted of them with a low-stress, fun approach. Once the dog learns what is wanted, but he chooses not to obey, then we can force him into the position to stay consistent, but initially there is no need for any negative reinforcement since he doesn't even know what is wanted of him in the first place.

Motivation

Your first step is to find what motivates your dog. A dog that is food motivated is by far the easiest dog to work with. Some dogs are not as motivated by food, but will still take food when they are in a familiar area, without distractions, and if they are hungry – if this is the case with your dog, we will start easy, and build our way up.

Other dogs are motivated by a favorite toy. For some it is a tennis ball, for others it is a toy that squeaks.

Some dogs are not motivated by food, or by toys, but all dogs love to be pet. Yes – all of them. You just need to find your dog's 'button'. The 'button' is wherever your dog really reacts to a good pet. It might be a scratch with the fingernails on the lower back, or a good firm rub behind the ears. Take a moment and give a doggie-massage to find your dog's button, and use it to your advantage.

Training Obedience for the Food Motivated Dog

Even if your dog is highly food motivated we are still going to do training right before meal time. If you have a highly food motivated dog, just use their regular kibble. If you have a dog that needs more enticement, use hot dogs. I prefer to use a healthier hot dog, like chicken, and cut it into pieces that are the size of the tip of a pencil eraser –

and for very small dogs, this can be even smaller. We want the treat to be just big enough that they can swallow it and be ready for the next one. We do not want to use biscuits that they are crunching, crumbs falling all over the floor, then the dog scavenging around to make sure he's got every last piece before he is ready for the next command.

Make sure to note how many treats your dog has had, and subtract that amount from his regular meal. For some dogs, the training session will take up their entire meal.

It is best to have training sessions several times a day, in short increments. Sessions that last maybe 3-5 minutes each, 3-5 times a day. Repetition is an important aspect to learning. Most dogs do not eat 3-5 times per day, but you should find that your dog will do better with his attention level in the lessons that are right before his regularly schedule meal time.

Dog's Name, Come, and Good Dog

This can be taught to dogs older than 5 weeks of age.

When teaching the dog's name we are only showing him that when he hears his name it means that we have something for him – we are not concerned about him knowing that his name is his identity. In this example, the dog's name is Max. Every time you say Max you will put a treat in front of his nose, then allow him to eat it. When you let go of the treat and it goes into his mouth say 'good dog'.

You can be sitting on the couch, watching television, and randomly say your dog's name, and put the treat down in front of his nose. When he takes it, say 'good dog'. This is something that you will want to practice with your dog throughout the day, and be as random as possible. The best way to practice this often is to have small candy dishes spread around your house with kibble sitting inside. Perhaps you will be washing your dishes, and look over and see the treats sitting there on the counter – you'll grab one and call out your dog's name, followed by 'come', even though your dog is in the other room. You will walk over to your dog, who may be sound asleep, repeat the name, and put the treat under his nose, and when he takes it say 'good dog'.

If your dog is already at your side you will only say his name, if he is further away from you say his name followed by 'come'. Example, 'Max, come'.

Eventually we want your dog to hear his name, and like a trigger it stops whatever he is doing and he turns to come to you.

We are doing two things here. We are teaching the dog that when you say his name he should come over to you and pay attention because you have something for him, and we are teaching him to associate the phrase 'good dog' as a positive.

While this seems very simple, it is also very difficult because you need to remain

100% consistent. It will be easy for you to say his name while you are talking to him – well, if you do, grab a treat real quick and show it to him. It will be very tempting to call him to you while you are trying to make a mad dash out the door – but if you do, you better grab a treat and show it to him.

Saying 'good dog' when he takes the treat is not as difficult, but it is a habit that you should get into. By doing this we are already working on weaning him off of treats. When he has learned to associate 'good dog' as a positive, you will be able to say it without a treat, and he will still have all those positive feelings flowing and may even drool. For now though, say it every single time he gets that treat from your hand.

After you have practiced this for a few days it is time to change it up a bit. If your dog is not by your side, and you call him, and he does not come over to you, walk over to him and put the treat under his nose and then back up while luring him to follow the treat. Retreat until you are back where you had originally called him. When he has followed you all the way back to the original location give him the treat and say 'good dog'. This begins to teach him that he will need to come to you to receive the treat.

Problem Solving; Some dogs are overly eager to take the treat out of your hand and snap at your fingers as they are taking it. The best way to solve this is to move your hand very slowly towards your dog and stare directly into your dog's eyes. Sometimes this alone will cause your dog to use more caution because it is not normal, and it makes him more cautious. If he still snaps at your hand use your palm and bump him on the nose just sharp enough that he looks surprised, but not afraid. This shows him that he should respect your hand because it bites too. It will not teach your dog to fear your hand – remember he really wants that treat and is already overly eager to grab at it. If he is still snapping at your hand it is because you are not being firm enough. There will be a level where your dog stops for a second to consider the situation. It is much better to start gentle and work your way up – this way you won't go too hard.

Teaching Watch Me

This can be taught to dogs older than 6 weeks of age.

This is a command that you can teach randomly throughout the day. You will say your dog's name and show them the treat, and then say 'watch me' and hold the treat up right between your eyes. You want the dog to stare at the treat initially for just a second then reward the dog with the treat, making sure to say 'good dog' when the dog gets the treat. Once your dog does well staring at the treat for a second, increase the time by having the treat up by your eyes, and then very slowly reaching the treat down to the dog. Because the treat is getting closer the dog is motivated to keep staring at the treat. To him it is more exciting because it is getting closer.

Later you will want to hold the treat up by your eyes for two seconds, then increase to three seconds, and so on, until it is up to 30 seconds or more. This needs to be done gradually or your dog will lose interest.

This command is used to get your dog's attention back on you. It may be used if you see something on the floor that your dog should avoid and not pick up. You just say watch me and redirect him to you until you have walked past the item. Or maybe your dog is very excited about another approaching dog, you can redirect him to you until the temptation passes.

With some other commands you will wean your dog off of treats after only a couple of weeks, but with this command you will initially use treats every time you say it for at least a month, and then you will use treats every other time for at least a year.

<u>Teaching Sit and Touch</u>

This can be taught to dogs older than 6 weeks of age.

Start off by having your dog on leash at your left side, say his name and show him the treat, then slowly lift the treat up above his nose and over his head towards his back. His eyesight should follow the treat and he will turn his head up. Usually the dog will sit at this point because it is easier to sit than to stand and follow the treat with his eyes. If he does not sit naturally, use your other hand and press down on his rear end. As soon as he sits reward him by giving him the treat and saying 'good dog' simultaneously.

Once he is rewarded for sitting it is time to move him forward a little so he is standing. Moving him so that he is standing allows you to teach him sit again.

You will first say his name to tell him you have the treat, and put the treat under his nose.

Next move the treat away from him and encourage him to follow the treat with his nose and body. While you are luring him say 'touch'. When he has moved far enough for you, reward him with the treat and say 'good dog'.

For example, say 'Max', with the treat under his nose, then 'touch' as you lure him forward a couple feet, and then 'good dog' when you let him take the treat.

Once he has moved forward as you have requested and you have rewarded him, put another treat in your hand and tell him to sit just as before. You will repeat these different commands several times, having him move forward just a bit each time.

As he gets better at luring you can lure him further than just a couple steps at a time; lure him in figure 8's, around you in a circle, or across the room. 'Touch' is a very useful command that is the basis for teaching other more complicated assistance dog tasks.

Problem Solving; Some dogs will jump up at the treat when learning the sit command. If they jump, tug on the leash at the same time and say 'no'. This is cause and effect. Your dog learns that when they exhibit the jumping behavior it is not pleasant, but it is pleasant when they sit. If your dog gets up from the sit immediately, that is okay at this point. It will be handled later.

<u>Teaching Down</u>

This can be taught to dogs older than 6 weeks of age.

Start with your dog in the sit position, on leash.

Next say your dog's name and put the treat to his nose, then very slowly lure the dog's nose to the floor. Don't go all the way down to the floor, just ask your dog to lower his head, then reward with the treat. Keep shaping this behavior, asking him to lower his head little by little until he needs to move his legs to start to lay down, and eventually his elbows will touch the floor.

Problem Solving; Some dogs will get up from the sit position when being lured by the treat. If they do this immediately pull the treat far away from them and hold it next to your chest to make it clear the treat has left them, and say 'no' at the same time. This is

negative in itself because the positive presence of the treat was taken away. Have the dog sit, and try again. You can also hold your dog's rear end down, while luring the front of his body to the floor until he understands how to coordinate his body enough to do it on his own.

Other dogs will refuse to move their front legs out of the way to follow the treat closer to the floor, and will just stare at the treat. Sometimes this is because they are confused, but other times it is because they are not motivated enough by the treat and are being lazy. This leaves you with a dog who will only go down halfway. With these dogs you can put pressure with your fingers directly behind either side of their shoulder blades. Right behind the dogs shoulder blades is a pressure point, that when gently squeezed, will force the dog to move away from the pressure and lay down. This is much easier than trying to push your dog to the floor.

Very dominant dogs will not agree to being forced into the down position. If your dog becomes aggressive at all in this process, he will not make a good service dog, and you will need to seek professional help just for the dog to remain a safe pet.

The commands we have gone over so far are all taught initially with positive motivation alone. Other commands require a combination of reward and correction to show the dog what is desired and not desired. We will expand on more commands once you have a better understanding of correction.

<u>Training Methodology</u>

    I have always stood on the firm belief that training should be a dog-friendly experience. Positive motivation should be used at every opportunity. Training should be fun for trainer, handler, and dog. If one becomes frustrated then the training session should stop. With most commands firm, but fair reinforcement is added only when the dog understands what behavior is wanted, but chooses not to follow through. This creates a dog who responds consistently to commands in all situations.

    When you call your dog, he should come to you with tail and head held high, happy to be by your side – not slinking towards you with his tail between his legs.

    Some trainers would like to command a dog with treats and praise alone – but this creates a dog who will respond only if the treat or praise is more positive than anything else that he would rather be doing.

For example, if you asked your dog to "sit" and "stay" at the park, he may respond well just to get the praise you have to offer him – but if he likes chasing cats, and one just happens to run across the street, he is faced with an immediate decision. Your dog is thinking, "Which is better – chasing that cat all over town with my tongue lolling out the side of my mouth and having the time of my life . . . or getting a taste of that treat in my

master's hand?" For most dogs it would be chasing the cat. He then breaks away from you and darts across the street after the cat – where he has a high chance of getting hit by a car. But if he had been through training that involved positive as well as negative reinforcement, he has two reasons to do what you tell him, and a negative and a positive usually outweigh the positive alone.

Dogs come from a social structure with a strong hierarchy. It would be unnatural for your dog to view life neutrally, without care of who is the alpha – who is to be dominant or submissive. If you do not take the lead, and become the alpha of your 'pack', your dog will either be insecure, or take that position himself. The latter can turn into a potentially dangerous situation.

In this book most commands are initially taught with positive motivation only. The dog is lured into certain positions, such as 'sit' or 'down', then is rewarded with either treats, a favorite toy, or verbal and physical praise. Only once the dog responds consistently to the positive, but chooses not to act, is the correction added.

Determining what level of negative reinforcement a dog needs is a very delicate task and should be approached with care. Some dogs will submit to authority with just a simple 'no' in a firm and low voice – but with most dogs a quick tug on the leash is all that is needed.

Unfortunately, there are a lot of trainers out there who prefer to "get the job done quickly" and are too hard on the dog. This creates an animal who responds out of fear, rather than one who is well-rounded with both positive motivation and low-level negative reinforcement.

You do NOT need to be a heavy-handed-tyrant for your dog to obey.
You very simply need to be the leader. When you issue a command the response is absolute.
You do not give your dog a
choice by asking him to do it.
You tell him that he will do it.
After all, it is a command
. . . not a request.

Correction and Consistency

This section teaches you when to correct.

You will want to correct your dog for not responding to the following commands;

Heel, Sit, Down, Stay, Wait, Come

You will also correct for unwanted behaviors, such as;

Jumping Up on people, windows, doors, counters, or forbidden furniture. As well as Barking, Digging, Chewing, Lunging, Mouthing or Nipping, Etc.

You will **not** correct for the following commands;

Touch, Watch Me, Alert, Under, Paws Up, Corner, Search

These commands need to be trained through positive reinforcement only because dominating or correcting your dog will not teach them to respond to these commands any better, and will only confuse them.

Before moving forward with training you will need to decide on one or more methods for correcting your dog. At our service dog school almost every dog is trained with all of the following options. The more methods you use to train your dog, the better, because it will always keep them surprised and interested in what it is that you have to communicate to them.

Head Halter; This is a good option for most dogs, although most dogs do not like the feel of it at first. The head halter is designed to easily guide the dog through the turning of the head – just like the halter on a horse you can control even a large animal through the gentle guidance of the head. Most dogs fight against the halter the first few times they wear it. Imagine that you had never worn socks before and then they were suddenly forced upon you. You wouldn't like it either initially, but with time wearing them would be totally natural.

When you first introduce your dog to the head halter only put it on for a second, give a treat, then take it off. You continue to do this repeatedly, gradually increasing the time you leave the halter on your dog, still giving a treat. Once you have worked your way up to a few seconds, take a few steps with your dog and put some pressure on the halter with the leash, then stop and treat. Increase the steps taken until you are walking through the house. Most dogs paw at the halter, but you should reach down and remove their paw to prevent injury. Dogs with dewclaws can scratch their muzzle or eyes in the process. Try to redirect your dog's attention by using the 'watch me' command or 'touch' command.

Be patient – most dogs adjust to the head halter within a week.

The head halter is the easiest training tool for walks. In fact, many untrained dogs can be walked successfully with a head halter because it prevents them from pulling too strongly.

To correct a dog with a head halter give a little tug on the leash that would pull the dog's head slightly to the side or down, but NEVER up. If the dog is already putting strain on the leash you will move your hand towards the dog very quickly to gain slack and then give a quick tug backwards. The tug needs to be quick and surprising to catch the dog's attention and this is also where the negative aspect comes in for the dog. They do not enjoy the surprise. With cause and effect they learn that with wrong choices you will consistently tug on the leash.

Where you hold onto the leash is important. The leash should be slack, but held close enough to the dog's halter that you only have to move your hand about 12 inches to tighten the leash. If you hold the leash too far away from the dog's halter you will have to move your hand 2-3 feet or more before the leash is tight enough to give a correction.

The benefits of the head halter are;
* You can easily control your dog with very little strength.
* You can keep your dog from sniffing the ground or picking something up off of the ground very easily with the halter.
* It is a less aggressive way to correct your dog because the tug is not, and should not be, as strong.
* This is a great option for dogs that have a soft trachea as it puts no strain on the throat.

The negatives of the head halter are;
* This cannot be used for dogs with shorter muzzles.
* Dogs do not like the feel of the halter initially.
* The halter is harder to use around the house. Many times when you let go of the leash, or if the dog is in a down stay under a table and you can't see them, the dog will slide the halter off their nose. This is not a problem with most head halters because they will still stay around the back of the dog's head and do not come off completely. You can easily slip it over the dog's nose again – however, the problem comes in when you have a dog that is a chewer because they will often destroy the halter within minutes of it being off their nose if they are unattended.

Chain Collar; The chain collar is the option used most by professional trainers. Another term given to this collar is 'choke chain' because it does cinch tighter with pressure. We will **not** be using the chain collar as a choke chain. There are some who use the collar in an abusive fashion by choking the dog and only releasing the pressure once the dog responds. This is far too egregious, cruel, and completely unnecessary. We will be using the collar to surprise the dog by a quick cinch and immediate release. The sound of the chain chinking as it cinches is also a good surprise to the dog.

The structure of a dog's neck is very different than that of ours. A dog's head is extended away from their body in a way that requires a great deal of muscle for support. A dog is also retrieving everything with their mouths which again requires a great deal of neck muscle support. Because of this most dogs do not have a sensitive neck like we do. However, there are quite a few breeds that are predisposed to soft tracheas.

It is recommended that you discuss this with your veterinarian. If your dog has a soft trachea we will not recommend any form of collar, training or otherwise, as it can cause serious damage to your dog.

Chain collars do not come with instructions, and unfortunately many owners believe that the idea behind the collar is that the dog will not pull if it is getting choked. As a result many owners walk their choking dogs down the street, simply thinking that their dog is dim witted for putting itself through all the pain. But a dog would never figure this out on their own. The chain collar does require proper training to be effective as I will explain here.

Using a chain collar incorrectly can harm your dog, but using one correctly will make the chain collar the best option for training. You will not want to leave the chain collar on your dog, in fact it would be best to remove the chain collar every time you remove the leash, and you never have either on your dog unless you are present and can keep an eye on your dog.

You will also never tug straight up on the chain collar, above and behind your dog's neck, as this will put too much pressure on the trachea. It is still unlikely to cause harm to a dog that has a solid trachea but it is always best to ere on the side of caution. When correcting with a chain collar you will either tug sideways, towards your knees, or past your knees to the right, or tug downward.

When you tug it needs to surprise the dog. It needs to be so fast that it is like the flick of a whip. The leash needs to be kept <u>absolutely</u> loose and slack, and then tightened quickly to cinch the collar closed, and then <u>immediately</u> opened back up again, returning the leash to its slack state. If your dog is already pulling and putting strain on the leash you will move your hand towards your dog quickly to slacken the leash, then tug to correct.

The most important part of using a chain collar is to tug with lightning-fast speed for a quick cinch, and **<u>immediate release</u>**.

And **<u>never</u>** keep the collar tight longer than the split second that it takes to correct for unwanted behaviors.

Where you hold onto the leash is important. The leash should be slack, but held close enough to the dog's collar that you only have to move your hand about 12 inches to tighten the leash. If you hold the leash too far away from the dog's collar you will have to move your hand 2-3 feet or more before the leash is tight enough to give a correction.

Chain collars come in varying sizes and strengths. The size is based on the length of the collar, and the strength is based on the thickness of the chain. You will want to choose the thinnest chain that will work for your size dog. The thinner the chain the more easily it will break with strain. This is potentially a hazard if your dog is not trained in a good recall (the come command). The perfect size of a chain collar is the shortest that will fit around your dog's head. We want the chain collar to sit up as high on the neck as possible, and the longer the chain, the further down on the neck it will naturally fall. It should be a little difficult to slip the collar over your dog's head, and when taking it off you should have to push one ear gently through at a time.

When putting the chain collar on it is important to not put it on backwards. Most will initially look at a chain collar and not see how it could possibly be put on wrong, but if put on backwards it will not release between corrections.

Start off by facing your dog head on, with your dog facing straight at you, as seen on the page 49. Then put the chain collar in the shape of a P, with the stem of the P coming straight down through the ring as demonstrated in the picture. Now slip the collar over your dog's head. It will not be in the shape of a P for your dog; it will be backwards for him because he is facing you. Now when your dog is on your left side, facing the same direction as you, the collar should automatically release when the leash is slack.

The benefits of using a chain collar are;
- It is more surprising to the dog than any other form of training collar and therefore gets a stronger reaction from the dog and it is very clear to them what is right and what is wrong.
- It is a good training collar to use while training house manners because he cannot slip it off when you are not looking.

The negatives of using the chain collar are:
- You cannot use the chain collar on dogs with soft tracheas.

Problem Solving;

If you have a breed that has a short muzzle and a soft trachea you cannot use a head halter or a collar. In this case you would be better off using a no-pull body harness. The best type would be one that has a clip for the leash attached to the front of the harness by the chest. You can still give quick sharp tugs as corrections, but it will not be as effective as it would if you were able to use a chain collar or head halter. You will correct the dog the same way with a body harness as you would with a head halter.

Squirt Bottle; This is an excellent option for use around the house. If your dog makes a poor choice you follow it up with a squirt of water towards their muzzle. This doesn't always work with dogs, but even most dogs who love water will not like the surprise of the squirt bottle. For example, if you asked the dog to sit, and he didn't, you would squirt him and say no, then repeat the command. If he were barking at the sound of the doorbell you would squirt him and say no.

The Leg Bump; It is very important that you understand we are not kicking the dog, but simply nudging the dog with the side of our leg. It's a quick nudge because we still want it to be a surprise, but it is the surprise that is negative, not the force behind your leg. No correction should ever hurt the dog, or make the dog afraid of you. The dog should have a respect for you and know that you are always consistent with your reinforcement of commands.

The Level of Correction

Inside your home, without distractions, your correction will usually be a very low level for you to get an obedient response from your dog. However, if you are out in public with distractions the correction level usually needs to be higher just for your dog to feel it.

When dogs get excited adrenaline begins to flow through their bodies. A good way for us to understand this is to compare it to an auto accident. You are probably aware that when people are in auto accidents they can be seriously injured, even have a limb severed, but not feel the injury right away. This is due to adrenaline. It is a survival mechanism that we are thankfully born with. For dogs something very similar happens to them when they get excited, and they are unable to feel what they normally would if they were relaxed. This is a survival mechanism for them as well and assists wild dogs who need to catch prey to survive, or helps them be stronger if they were injured during a fight.

For example, let's say you are using a chain collar with your dog as soon as you walked out the door for a walk. Your dog is thrilled because of the change of environment and his adrenaline spikes. You will need to tug considerably harder for your dog to feel anything at all.

The best way to find the right level of correction is to always start at the lowest level your dog responds to at home, then gradually increase the level of your correction until he responds. This way you will not come on too strong. Your dog will respond before he feels pain – he will respond when it is uncomfortable.

This next paragraph will make all the difference in the world when training your dog.

In order for training to be effective you must constantly annoy your dog until he does comply. If you tell him to sit and he does not, you must immediately follow this with a correction, then give the command again, followed immediately by a stronger correction, followed by the command again, and then proceeding to an even stronger correction and so on. If you wait between corrections he is getting away with it. He needs to be constantly annoyed until he complies. You must also continuously increase the level of your correction each time until you find the right level for that moment of specific distraction. If the first correction didn't work it is because he either did not feel it, or because he is not motivated enough to follow through due to the level of the correction.

It is important to remember to view life through the eyes of your dog. If you are too hard on your dog he will become fearful and stressed. It may appear for a moment that it solved the behavior because he stopped - however he stopped because he shut down. A dog that is stressed is not learning anything - it is simply delaying the inevitable.

Advanced Obedience

An Advanced Sit and Down

If your dog is at the point where he is responding consistently with treats for the sit and down command it is time to start weaning him off. At first you will give him treats every other time, then every third time, and so on. You will still say 'good dog' when he responds correctly. If you have trained him correctly, by saying 'good dog' each time he has gotten a treat in the past, you will see that he is still happy when he hears the phrase, even if a treat is not involved. I would still encourage you to give your dog a good pet or scratch when you praise, it is just that the treat is not always present any longer.

Now that your dog clearly understands what it is you are asking him to do, there will still be times when he chooses not to obey. Most of the time it is because there is something else he would rather be doing, but some of the time it is because he is simply being stubborn and is trying to be the leader himself.

When he chooses not to respond to your commands you will correct him. You will not give the command twice before correcting him – expect that he respond after the first time you give the command. How you correct him will vary on the method used, but in all cases a correction is something only negative enough that he would work to avoid it, but not be afraid of it.

When you tell your dog to sit and he does not, you will wait no longer than a split second and then correct him. You must then immediately give the command again. If he still does not comply immediately follow through with a second correction, only at a higher level this time, and then give the command again.

The reason we are giving the command after each correction is because it is possible that he legitimately did not hear you or was too distracted to hear you, so we are giving him a second chance now to catch on. If you think he truly did not hear you, correct him anyway. You are already being clear and concise when you issue the command; you are saying his name and using a hand signal. If he did not hear you, he will do better to listen the next time. The reason you need to correct him the first time, every time, is that you need to remain totally consistent. Most dogs are excellent actors. They are very good at looking like they did not hear you. Some will stare across the yard, some will even stare at you with a confused look – but as long as they truly understood these commands with treats, they are just playing you.

Your dog does not need to be looking at you to hear the command, or even to be looking at your hand signal – they still know what to do. When you tell your dog to down and he does not, you will correct him. If you are correcting with a tug on the leash it is best to tug downward if you can because that is the direction we want him to go. This is what I call a directional correction. It will make more sense to the dog.

Another way to correct him downward without bending over is to hold a slack leash in your hand, and then step on the leash somewhere in the middle so that the dog is pulled down towards your foot and the ground. You will still need to step on the leash quickly enough that it surprises the dog, because we certainly don't expect you to pull the dog down with the weight of your foot. In fact most of the time your foot is not touching the ground when it taps on the leash, it is just pushing down on the leash for a split second and then letting up again – very similar to a leash correction given by hand; quick and then followed by immediate release. Like the flick of a whip.

For down you can also use a lower voice, and draw it out so it sounds similar to a growl. This is because you are asking the dog to show you a submissive position. For dogs laying down is similar to one human bowing down or kneeling in front of another – it is a sign of respect and honor. When you lower your voice like a growl you are not being mean to your dog, you are communicating in a way they naturally understand. It is clear to the dog that you are trying to assert your authority and that you are being domineering while telling him to down.

Because down is a naturally submissive position, your dog may start to lay down for you when you say sit – but this is okay. According to your dog he is showing you respect when he lays down, so if you say sit, and he lays down he is actually paying you a compliment. However, if you told your dog to down, and he only sat, he is not doing as much as what you have asked him to do, and you should correct him and make him lay down.

Just like with the sit command we will correct him within a split second for not following through, followed by another command, then followed by a stronger correction, and so on.

In this more advanced stage of training we will also start correcting the dog for not staying in the sit or down position. At this stage we are starting to teach the dog that when you say sit or down that you mean to stay in that position until you tell him to do otherwise. (The exception to this is if you said sit, and he sat and then lay down. This would be acceptable because he is still doing what you have asked.) If you say sit and he sits for only a second and pops back up, you will immediately correct him and tell him to sit again. If your dog pops up from a sit do not simply tell him to sit again – you must correct first, and then redirect to sit.

If your dog is having trouble staying in the down position in this early stage you can step on the leash right after the clip so that if your dog did try to get up, he couldn't. If he manages to still stand, while keeping the front of his body to the ground with your foot and the leash, you will simply reach down and push behind his shoulder blades to make him lay back down again. Within a few tries of this he will realize it is just more comfortable to stay down.

With a service dog you will be very mobile together, and when you go into public he will be laying down almost every time you stop. Because of this we want him to learn that when you say down he does so immediately without question, and then stays in the down position until you start to move forward again. You do not have to say stay for him to stay in the down position, however once you start moving that is his cue to get up. Now, if you wanted to move away from him and didn't want him to follow, you would say stay before you started to move away. We will work on stay later.

At this stage of training you can also start teaching down from a standing position. He has already mastered it from a sit, but now needs to learn it straight from a stand. You will practice this just as you did from the sit, only he will have a much better understanding and should accomplish this with little trial. Some dogs will leave their rear end standing in the air while their elbows are flat on the ground. In this case simply push his rear end down and he will realize that is much more comfortable – practice makes perfect.

<u>Teaching Heel</u>

This can be taught to dogs older than 12 weeks of age.

If you have a dog that has never been leash trained, tart by having your dog wear a flat collar that does not cinch tighter, and attach the leash. The important part here is that your dog is not afraid of being attached by the leash. A dog that is afraid will rear and buck and pull backwards with all their might – do not let them pull you with them;

you must stand solidly still. They must learn that pulling away will not help. You can get down and comfort and pet them – we don't want this to be a traumatic experience. Your dog should begin to feel comfortable with the leash within a couple sessions.

Heel is a moving command. We are teaching the dog that when you say 'heel' it means that you are going to move, and that he is going to come along with you, no exceptions. You will take a step forward and say your dog's name followed by 'heel'. Make sure to show him that you have the treat when you say his name. Once you start moving you must be like a locomotive that is not going to stop! Many handlers are tempted to stop and have a conversation with their dog about why they should come along – but this topic is not up to discussion. Your dog will learn quickly that when you say 'heel' and move forward that it is simply time to go. If your dog is truly struggling to keep up (not pulling ahead or to the side, but keeping up) and it is clear that he is not tired or too young, use a flat collar that does not cinch tighter, and pull him along with you. Your dog will struggle and drag his feet for a bit, but will quickly learn that he should just move his feet and keep up. When he does, give him a treat, but keep up your pace and be moving forward when you give the treat. Remember that if you have followed the steps outlined in this guide your dog already knows to come to you when you call his name. If you call his name he should be willing to keep up and come with you.

In the beginning lessons you will give him a treat every ten feet or so, but keep moving, don't stop. Once he is coming along with you for the treat it is time to change to the training collar, training harness, or head halter.

Timing is most important when teaching this more advanced session of heel. When a dog is learning to heel it is all about cause and effect. The dog learns that when they are walking by your side it is positive, and when they are not it is negative.

You can start off with the dog on any side of you, or even to the front or back of you – but when you say 'heel' you start moving and pull your dog over to walk on your left.

You want your dog's shoulders to be even with your hip. It does not matter where their feet are, or where your feet are because as you are moving so are your feet. You also want to imagine a hula hoop going around your waist and around your dog. If your dog leaves the circumference of that invisible hula hoop he is too far away. If his shoulders leave your hip, he is too far away. You **must** correct him the **second** he leaves your side otherwise he will never understand where you want him to be.

If you walk in a straight line at the same pace, your dog will do poorly. But if you change your pace and turn constantly he is forced to watch you. If you turn and he looses you, he gets corrected.

You can start off by walking forward 5 feet and making an abrupt about turn to go the opposite direction, if he looses you he gets corrected. If he does not come with you he gets corrected. Go back and forth in a 5 foot span for a full minute, turning again every 5 feet, correcting him each time he does not come with you. Some dogs learn to turn

when you turn within a few tries, but others will take a few lessons. Remember, that if the correction is not hard enough he has no motivation to turn with you; if it is a light tug you are only physically manipulating him to come with you and there is no negative for him if he does not come on his own, which means he will continue to ignore you because he has no reason to pay attention.

After you have made about turns, change it up. Now you can walk forward a few feet, and then stop. Do not say anything to your dog when you stop, just stop. If he does not stop, you correct him. If his shoulders

leave your hip even the slightest inch, you will correct him. Within a few tries he will understand that he gets tugged if he goes ahead of you. Next walk forward a few feet then turn abruptly to your right and tug if he does not follow. Then turn to your left. If he does not back out of your way while you are turning in his direction you will bump him with your knee; just a nudge to make him respect your personal space.

Because this has many opportunities for mistakes on your dog's part he will receive many corrections. To keep the session positive make sure to offer him treats for walking along by your side. You can also use the 'watch me' command and reward him for watching you as you go.

The more you correct your dog, the more you need to reward him. Sometimes you will need to find reasons to reward him, possibly even rewarding him for extremely simple things that he mastered ages ago – but we do not want to get his spirits down with too much negative. After all, if he is not having fun, neither are you.

<u>Teaching Stay</u>

Start with your dog in the sit position. He should be wearing his training collar, harness or halter, while you hold onto the leash. Before you move away from him you put your palm directly in front of his face and say stay. Do not say his name before stay. Before when you have said his name it encourages him to come to you, but now we do not want him to follow you. You will only take one step away from him and then step back and praise him. If he gets up to follow you, correct him and tell him to sit and stay again.

At first you only take one step away, then move back. Once he is good at this you will back further away until you are at the end of the leash. Gradually increase the time you stay at the end of the leash, always returning to praise. The praising does not show the dog what to do as the timing will not make sense to him. You are praising him because you do not want him to hate the stay command. The stay command is already negative to the dog because you are not allowing him to be with you, and the best way for him to learn to stay is by correcting him when he gets up.

Once he is doing well with you backing away directly in front of him, you will walk back and forth in front of him until you are walking in a U shape, with him in the center. Once he does this well you can walk around him in full circle. This is harder for the dog because he wants to follow you with his eyes and it is difficult to do that with you walking in a full circle behind him.

Once he does well at this level you can drop the leash, but be sure to jump back towards him and correct with the leash whenever he gets up.

He can lay down if he gets tired. And after he

does well with a sit stay you can graduate to a down stay. But if you tell him to do a down stay he cannot get up to a sit.

The down stay is not necessarily given to the dog to make him submissive, but that is how he will take it naturally. The down stay is usually better than a sit stay because it is easier for the dog to relax in this position and it is harder for him to get up quickly.

Before having your dog do a down stay in public you will want to make sure he can do long stays within your home. Have him stay while you are eating dinner or watching television. Service dogs are required to do long down stays on most public outings so this is something important to master. When he is doing a long down stay he can stretch and switch from side to side, but he needs to do all of this while laying down – he cannot stand or sit up at any point. If he starts to crawl forward you will want to correct him.

You will also want to proof your dog. Proofing your dog is adding distractions and temptations to your training session to make sure he can handle the excitement of the real world out in public. You may throw his favorite toys around the room while he is in a down stay, or even kneel down a few feet in front of him to see if he will get up. If you can have other dogs or children run and play around him that would be ideal, but in many cases you would have to go to a park to practice this.

Our end goal is that your dog will be able to do a stay for at least a couple of hours. I realize this is a lot to shoot for initially, but there will be many situations where you will need your dog to stay that long; outings to movie theaters, plays, restaurants, work, school, etc..

<u>Teaching Wait</u>

Wait and stay are two totally separate commands. Stay means not to move out of one spot, while wait means to not go past a certain boundary. For example, if you were going out your front door to the car, and you didn't want your dog to follow you, you could say 'wait' at the door. This means he cannot go past the boundary of the door, but he can turn around and go somewhere else in the house if he wishes. However, if you told him to stay at the front door, he better be in that exact spot when you get back.

You will use 'wait' at all doorways. As soon as you reach for the handle you tell your dog to 'wait'. If he tries to dart out the door you will tug on his leash if he is wearing one, or you can bump him with the side of your leg, or even squirt him with a squirt bottle. He can then proceed through the door as soon as you start walking through it, but he needs to walk by your side in the heel position and cannot go ahead of you.

This is imperative because dogs consider themselves as the leader when they go through small spaces in front of you. Even if you were walking in a narrow space, say between two clothing wracks in a shop, you would need to tell your dog to wait so he will walk single file behind you. This is also an important safety issue. Obviously it creates safety issues when a dog darts through doorways out into the street, but service dogs often go into elevators with their handlers. We would never want the chance of the dog entering an elevator before you and having the doors close you out on the opposite side. If the elevator was called you may not know where to retrieve your dog.

Teaching Good House Manners

The best way to remain consistent with your dog in the house is to always have your dog wearing his leash when you are present. You will not need to hold onto the leash; just let it drag behind your dog through the house. This way you can easily correct any unwanted behaviors.

Jumping Up

It is natural for dogs to jump up, but they still must learn that it is not acceptable unless they are invited up in a form of training.

For example if the doorbell is ringing you can prepare for the fact that your dog may try to jump up on the guests and make sure he is wearing a leash. When your dog jumps up on your guest tug back on the leash strong enough that he chooses not to jump any longer.

If your dog has trouble jumping up on you when you enter the house, be sure to have a squirt bottle waiting just outside the door. When you walk inside hide the bottle behind your back. You don't want him to know when you have it, otherwise he will be good when he sees the bottle, but still jump up when he doesn't.

The trainers at our school often carry squirt bottles hanging off the backs of their belts as they are working in the kennel - they never know when they might need to surprise a jumping dog. Consistency is the key.

In some situations you may need to set your dog up. In the example of counter surfing you may have to show your dog that you are putting crackers on the counter, and then pretend to leave, while in actuality you are spying on your dog to see when he jumps up so you can run in and correct him.

If your dog does jump up make sure to say 'no' when you correct, and don't say 'down' unless you plan to make your dog lay down.

Getting on the Furniture

Proper service dog etiquette does not allow dogs to be up on furniture in public, therefore it is best to teach your dog to stay off the furniture at home. If you want to allow your dog to sleep in your bed with you it will be more confusing initially, but in time he will understand the difference between one piece of furniture and all the rest, as long as you are consistent.

If your dog hops up or even puts their front feet on a forbidden piece of furniture you will correct him and say no. Do not say down because this means to lay down.

Proofing your Recall

The term 'recall' refers to the command of calling your dog to you. Even though you will continue to use treats for the come command long after it is consistent, there still may be times that your dog would prefer to do something more exciting than getting the treat you have to offer. To keep recalls consistent you will want to have your dog wear a long line when they are roaming or playing outdoors. A long line is a lightweight lead that is ten feet or longer. You will want to use a long line that is no shorter than fifteen to twenty feet, depending on your needs. The long line will drag behind him just as his regular leash as used inside the house. You will not pick the leash up unless you need to correct him.

If your dog is roaming or playing wait until he is interested in something other than you and then call him. Make sure to use the exact command and tone of voice that you have always used before. You will also want to have the treat just as you always have before. But now if he does not turn to come to you within a split second you will reach down and tug on the long line and say no, then follow it up by the recall command.

If your dog has moved so far away from you that the long line is out of reach you would do best to wait to until you are holding the line before you call your dog at all.

Even if you do have to correct your dog when he does not come to you, you will still want to reward him once he gets to you.

Public Access

The Laws that Protect Your Rights

The ADA does not specify that service dogs must be certified, or even that they need to be trained by a professional. But they do need to be well behaved and need to be trained in specific tasks to assist their disabled handler's specific disability.

Be sure to check frequently for any updates to the ADA. It is your responsibility to know your rights.

AMERICANS WITH DISABILITIES ACT
DEFINITION OF A SERVICE ANIMAL
ADA Subpart A 36.104 Definitions - Final Rule Title III
Service animal means any dog that is individually trained to do work or perform tasks for the benefit of an individual with a disability, including a physical, sensory, psychiatric, intellectual, or other mental disability. Other species of animals, whether wild or domestic, trained or untrained, are not service animals for the purposes of this definition. The work or tasks performed by a service animal must be directly related to the handler's disability. Examples of work or tasks include, but are not limited to, assisting individuals who are blind or have low vision with navigation and other tasks, alerting individuals who are deaf or hard of hearing to the presence of people or sounds, providing non-violent protection or rescue work, pulling a wheelchair, assisting an individual during a seizure, alerting individuals to the presence of allergens, retrieving items such as medicine or the telephone, providing physical support and assistance with balance and stability to individuals with mobility disabilities, and helping persons with psychiatric and neurological disabilities by preventing or interrupting impulsive or destructive behaviors. The crime deterrent effects of an animal's presence and the provision of emotional support, well-being, comfort, or companionship do not constitute work or tasks for the purposes of this definition.

Local state laws will provide other provisions to protect your rights and those of the general public. Be sure to check your state's regulations regarding service dogs, however keep in mind that the local laws are there to give you more rights; to offer further protection. In any case where local law and Federal law disagree, the Federal law will supersede.

The following tips and training will enable your experiences in public with your dog to be positive. Your dog will need to be accustomed to working in elevators, walking next to grocery carts, and being well behaved in the close confines of public bathroom stalls.

Loading and Unloading from the Vehicle

When it is time to load into the vehicle tell your dog to 'sit' and 'wait' before you put your hand on the door handle. Say 'wait' very clearly. You can even stare at him a little longer than normal so he knows you are very serious. If he tries to dart in as you are opening the door, correct him and start over. After you open the door do not immediately tell him to get in. Wait a little longer to build his patience. After you are sure he is waiting for your cue, tell him 'inside' and lure his nose into the vehicle with a treat.

Some dogs need a little help stepping up into larger vehicles. We like to use a storage tub turned upside down. These are better than steps made specifically for dogs as they are lighter, cheaper, and the storage tubs can be used to hold groceries and other loose items once inside the car, to keep them from rolling into your dog.

To use the tub simply turn it upside down and step on the lip of the tub with both feet, one foot on each side of the tub. This is to keep it from slipping out from under your dog's feet. You may need to lure your dog onto the tub slowly, first only luring his nose over the tub with a treat, followed by a reward. Each training session should move further ahead, asking your dog to put the front feet on the tub, and then the back feet on the tub as he heads into the vehicle. Make sure to use lots of treats in this process, rewarding for each small step forward.

When he is traveling in your personal vehicle it would be best to have him confined. You can use a seatbelt system designed for dogs and sold at pet stores, or you can use a body harness which you have attached to the non-retractable seatbelt in your back seat with an extremely short leash. You can use his service dog vest with the leash attached to the ring if you prefer.

Remember that airbags can hurt your dog just as easily as they can hurt a child. Using a crate is another safe alternative, but if you choose this route make sure it is well secured. A loose dog in an auto accident would not only have the risk of going through the windshield, but could also become a projectile that would kill you on impact.

If you have trouble getting him close enough to his seatbelt to buckle him in, remember to use your 'touch' command to lure him closer.

Proper training in unloading is very important. The few seconds in which you are unloading your dog from a vehicle is the moment he is preparing to either behave for you throughout your adventure into public, or to do his own thing. We obviously want him focused on you.

Keep in mind that while you are practicing this training at home, that in a real situation he will have been in the car for a matter of minutes or even hours, you have finally stopped the car, and now he is excited to get out and see where you have taken him. His first concern is not naturally to focus on you, but to see what adventures await him outside the car.

Once you have opened the door to take your dog out of his safety restraint system, tell him to 'down' and 'stay' before you release him from his seatbelt or open his crate door. In the beginning he is likely to refuse. This is because you probably taught him to 'down' on the ground, and now all of a sudden he is elevated at a different height. Correct him if he refuses, and show him what you want him to do.

Initially you may need to correct him several times because this is all very exciting to him.

If you are relieving him from a safety restraint system, make sure to put his leash on first. If he darts out of the car at the sound of his seatbelt being loosened, you may loose your dog, or worse. Remember you are in a parking lot – or will be in a real situation.

Problem solving for crates;
If he is in a crate, tell him to 'wait' before opening the crate door. If he darts, close the door on him. It may bump his nose. When done at the right level this will not hurt him, but will deter him and teach patience. Once the door is open put his leash on and tell him to 'down' and 'stay'.

Once your dog is in a 'down stay' you will say 'stay' again before backing up. You are reiterating this to him because you know he is extra excited to get out, and when you are backing up it will seem to him like your body language is telling him to get out of the car.

Once you have backed up enough for him to hop out of the car, tell him to 'stay' again. You can never teach him enough patience.

When you are sure he is paying attention to you, put a treat in your hand and point to the ground and say 'out'. As he is on his way out of the car, put the treat in front of his nose and lure him to the ground, but then immediately lure his nose back up into the sit position. This is important! You want him to be focused on YOU as soon as his feet touch the ground. We don't even want to give him the opportunity to be excited about his surroundings. You are to be his focus, and you alone.

Once he is watching you, give him the treat and say 'good dog'. Then immediately put him into the heel position and walk SLOWLY away from the car and to your destination. If you are walking slowly he has to focus on you even harder just to stay by your side. This is another tactic in keeping him focused on you, on his obedience, and his motivation, instead of his new surroundings.

Elevators, Stairs, and Escalators

Always have your dog wait a little longer than usual before entering the elevator. In fact, it may be a good idea to even let your dog watch the elevator door open on various occasions, and then close without getting on at all. You can also give him the 'watch me' command as the door opens. Many dogs are very anxious to go through doorways – they can't wait for what is on the other side. But in the case of elevators this is even more dangerous than usual. What if you were having trouble getting into the elevator yourself because of extra baggage, or what if you were turned around talking to someone and didn't notice the elevator door open at all? Your dog would notice, hop in, and likely end up on a different floor, leaving you guessing where he got out. You can never instill enough patience in your dog.

Once you are in the elevator tell him to 'down'. Some dogs don't like the feeling of the elevator rising so it helps to have them in a 'down'.

Be aware that many people who are coming into the elevator on other floors are not looking down, so may not see that you have a dog. It is your duty to keep others from stepping on your dog.

Never take your dog on an escalator for safety. His feet and tail can get stuck in the teeth.

If you are forced to use a moving walkway always leave space between you and the people in front of you. This is because you will want to pick up your pace and jog off the walkway when it ends. This will lift your dog's feet and tail up higher, greatly reducing the chance of him getting caught up.

When using the stairs always be sure to hold onto the hand rail. This is an extremely important safety precaution. Even once your dog is trained to go up and down stairs with you well, it still doesn't take a lot for him to trip on him and fall.

When working with your dog on stairs keep in mind that it is difficult for your dog to go down because he is top heavy. Because of this he will want to go faster than you.

In the initial phases of training with stairs always go very slowly. This is to teach him to focus on your pace and to have patience himself. At first it will be difficult for him to stay with you, but he will learn that a correction will occur when his front feet are not on the same step as your feet. In the beginning it may help to take one step forward every 2 seconds, stop completely, then continue to the next step.

Grocery Carts and Strollers

Anytime you are pushing something your dog will view that object as an extension of you. Don't be surprised when they walk up by the object and leave your side, even in 'heel'. You will need to make some left turns so that your dog moves out of the way. Don't run him over or let his toes get stuck in the wheels, but he needs to see the cart coming his way so he can watch out for it.

It is best to rest your palm against the handle of the cart or stroller, and let the pressure of your palm against the handle hold the leash in place. If you try to hold the leash and push the cart one-handed you will have problems. This is awkward initially, but hold the leash the way this book suggests and you will be happier in the long run.

If your dog is afraid of the cart you may want to work with a stroller or something smaller at home. You want to push it on a surface that makes the cart silent, and walk slowly. If your dog is still having trouble put some treats next to the wheels of the cart and let your dog eat them. Next balance the treats on the cart somehow so he can eat them right off the cart. Hold onto the cart tight when he is taking the treats – we don't

want it moving suddenly if he bumps it.

Eventually you can move the cart to louder surfaces and he will be fine.

Restroom Stalls

Proper restroom etiquette for service dogs? Yes, it exists. At least it does with Little Angels. Have you ever had a child look under your restroom stall? Many people react the same way when a dog sticks his nose under the partition to watch them doing their business. Don't let this be your dog.

If you are using a stall in the lavatory, you will find it useful to use the stall made with wheelchair access. This stall is larger so it will accommodate both you and your dog, and there are handrails along the sides put there for

mobility assistance. These rails are an excellent hitching post for your dog while your hands are otherwise occupied. Just tie your dog's leash to the rail so he can't put his head down far enough to look into the neighboring stall. This also helps to keep him from laying down on the dirty floor.

The protocol used when washing your hands, or when using the urinal, is the same. You make the leash taught enough that your dog cannot put his head down, then wrap the leash around your elbow twice to secure it as seen in the picture on the following page. This gives you control over your dog, while allowing you to have free use of both hands. You can use this method anytime you need both hands free.

Checkout Lines

Whenever you are in any line you should still always have your dog do a 'down stay' any time you are not moving. This may look like doggie push-ups when you take a step forward and your dog gets up to follow you, then lays right back down again. It may initially seem like overkill, but it is a good habit to get into. Take into account that you may be distracted and your dog is surrounded by snacks and candy right at nose level. Snacks are put there purposefully to attract children specifically, so it will do the same for your dog. He is less likely to be pulling things off the shelves if he is in a 'down stay' with your foot resting securely on the leash.

When you reach the register the clerk will likely greet you. Don't let this distract you from telling your dog to 'down'. Initially this is a hard habit to get into. Many handlers feel pressured to talk to the clerk before telling their dog to down. Don't let this happen to you. Smile at the clerk when they greet you, but be telling your dog to 'down'. They will see you have a dog and will understand.

If you need to use both hands to dig through your wallet or sign a check, make sure to wrap the leash around your elbow.

Another option is to step on the leash, putting your foot right below the leash's clip. Then you will slide your wrist through the loop of the leash. This is another way of making sure your dog is close at hand while still having your hands free. This is the option I usually use when indoors, because if I stop, my dog is going into the down position.

<u>Giving your Dog Water</u>

I like to travel light. When you get a service dog vest, do yourself a favor and get one that has a zippered pocket.

You can keep potty bags in there, as well as your wallet and keys if you choose to.

Instead of carrying around a separate water bowl for my dogs I have gotten creative. I always purchase potty bags that are scent free and powder free. I fold the

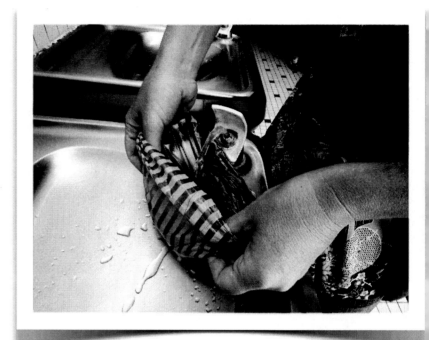

sides of the bag down and fill it with water at a drinking fountain, and teach my dogs to drink out of it.

Anytime you drink something while you are out and about, think about your dog too. He is probably just as thirsty as you are. Offer him water out of the clean potty bag. If you would like to save the bag for further use, just fold it up and put it right back into the zippered pocket of his service dog vest.

Assistance Dog Tasks

Everyone's disability effects them differently. Some of you will be able to use all of the tasks in this book, and others will only need a few. The important part in selecting tasks is to make sure that it is worth the time and effort put into training, based on the usefulness of the trained task in the end.

We could never include all the tasks a dog can do for you in one book, however if you need a task that is not listed you will easily be able to take what you have learned in this book and convert the training to suit your needs.

Under

This is an important task that almost every service dog will need to know. It is not useful in assisting with your disability, but under is used to tell the dog to go under tables, desks, benches and chairs. It is essential that larger dogs can be out of the way in crowded public places. When you are seated at a restaurant the host takes you to your table. The host will know you have a service dog, but when the waiter approaches they are not expecting a dog and cannot always see the floor due to the serving trays they are often carrying. If your dog is sitting next to your chair he may get stepped on, but if he is tucked under the table he is safe from any unknowing traffic.

The under command is a rendition of the touch command. With touch your dog has been trained to follow your hand with his nose until you release the treat. With under you are luring the dog under the table with your hand and the treat, and when he is under you will tell him to 'down', and 'stay'.

Under a Table or Desk
1)   Walk up to the table with the dog   in the heel position on your left side.
2)   Sit in your chair.
3)   Say your dog's name and show him the treat.
4)   Say 'touch' and lure your dog slowly under the table or desk.
5)   Hold onto the treat – the dog does not get it yet.
6)   Once your dog is completely under the table or desk tell him to 'down' and use the hand signal for down with the hand that still has the treat.
7)   Once the dog lays down release the treat into his mouth and say 'good dog'.
8)   Step on the leash with your right food, right under the buckle of the leash so the dog cannot get up even if he tried.
9)   Once you are ready to get up from the table or desk it is very important to tell your dog to stay. Be very clear. Your dog will be tempted to get up since he has been on a stay for perhaps an hour or more and you are suddenly getting up.
10) Do not call your dog until you are standing and have gathered everything that you need (such as your purse or shopping bags if in a restaurant). I like to train my dogs in this step by fidgeting and moving the chairs around a bit before actually calling them.
11) Call your dog by name, followed by heel and immediately walk away.

After your dog is following your hand under the table with the command of 'touch' you can switch the vocal cue to 'under'. Over time you will be able to point under the table and say 'under' and he will understand what to do without you actually luring him.

Under a Chair or Bench
1)   Initially you may need to kneel or bend over next to the chair or bench to lure the dog underneath.
2)   Say the dog's name and show him the treat.
3)   Say 'touch' and lure the dog under the furniture.
4)   Once he is totally under you will tell him to 'down'.
5)   Once he is down you release the treat into his mouth and say 'good dog'.
6)   Tell him to stay.
7)   If you will be sitting on the chair or bench it would be best to step on the leash right after the buckle so that your dog cannot stand up even if he tried.
8)   Before you stand tell him to stay, and be very clear.
9)   After you stand wait a moment before calling him up.
10) Call your dog's name, followed by 'heel' and walk away.

After your dog is doing well with this task you can change the vocal cue from 'touch' to 'under'. With repetition all you will need to do is point and say 'under' for your dog to understand exactly what you want.

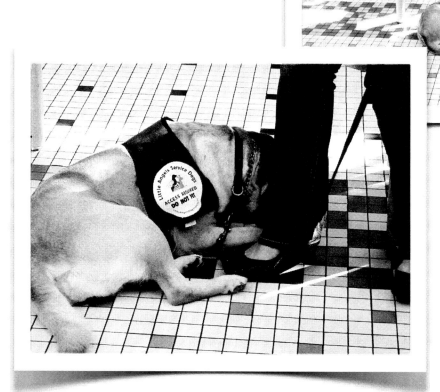

Assistance with Boundary Control

This task is used to assist those who need a larger area of personal space in crowded areas. It is common for the public to crowd in close to each other in smaller spaces such as grocery store lines, or elevators. In these cases the dog is used to create a barrier or boundary between you and other people.

We are not training the dog to protect you, and that is important to understand. For a dog to have public access he should be free of liability. If the dog had it in his head that he should protect you he would actually be a very high liability. Dogs that display the slightest sign of aggression should not be used for public access. These dogs could still assist someone medically in the home, but should not be taken into public. Remember that if your dog injured someone in public you have not only been responsible for that person's injury, but you will be held legally liable, and your dog can be taken from you and put down.

When we have a dog create a barrier of personal space for you, we are simply telling the dog to move as directed and to stay there. The dog does not understand why he is asked to comply with the task – he is doing so because you told him to.

You will want to practice this task at home first, then in public situations without crowds, and eventually ask him to perform the task with crowds, when you actually need the assistance.

Start with your dog on your left side in the heel position, or with him directly in front of you. Say his name and hold the treat in front of his nose, then say 'touch' and lure him to a different position somewhere around your body. For example you may have him start off in front of you, and then lure him to your right side, or directly behind you. When he has moved to the requested position tell him to 'down'. Correct him if he starts to move to another location to lay down. He needs to lay down exactly where you put him. Do not give him the treat until he is laying down. Then tell him 'good dog' and release the treat into his mouth. Then you will tell him to stay.

If there was someone standing close to you they would be forced to step back as you lure the dog between yourself and the other person. That person can no longer move any closer to you because your dog is blocking their path. This all seems very polite to those observing you; they do not know that you moved the dog between you due to your discomfort, or because you want that person farther away.

Many handlers will always choose to have the dog 'touch' and stay behind them in line. This will keep anyone joining the line to stay further back from you. They cannot go past the boundary created by the dog's body. When the line moves forward tell the dog to 'heel' and step forward. Then face the dog and tell them to 'down' directly behind you, just as before. You can be specific about how the dog's body is angled if you wish by using the 'touch' command. After you tell the dog to stay you can face forward again, resting assured that no one can come closer to you from behind, due to your dog's position.

Many dogs will wag their tails and seem genuinely happy that other people are standing so close to them. A dog that is still in the beginning phases of training may try to get up from the 'down stay' when another person talks to them. This happens often. Simply correct your dog and tell him to 'down stay' again. He will learn that he cannot get up, even when others are speaking to him.

<u>Medical Alert</u>

Dogs can be trained to perform tasks based off of command, or even off of association. For example, dogs have been taught to detect various forms of cancerous cells in medical patients. In training these dogs are presented with the scent of cancerous skin cells in a test tube. Each time the dog is presented with this scent the dog is told to sit, and then is rewarded for sitting. Other scents will be presented to the dog, but the dog is not told to sit. If he sits without the correct scent he is not rewarded. After much repetition the dog has learned to sit for the correct scent, even without the command to sit, and is thus rewarded. In this way dogs are tasked to scent out various patients. Some with cancer, and some without. When the dog detects the cancerous skin cells he will sit – then the trainer knows the dog has detected cancer in the patient.

Dogs are trained in this same way to detect explosives, guns, drugs, food allergens, people, termites, bed bugs, etc..

Little Angels Service Dogs goes beyond that and trains the dogs to recognize other signs from the body such as seizures, high or low blood sugar, high or low blood pressure, panic attacks, anxiety attacks, flashbacks, etc..

There have not been enough studies to determine how the dogs detect panic attacks, anxiety attacks, or flashbacks, but we believe it is a chemical scent that comes from the body of the disabled handler.

If you suffer from panic attacks, anxiety attacks, or flashbacks you are well aware that these can get out of hand very quickly. If you train your dog to alert you of an attack, you can be immediately redirected to your dog before the condition escalates.

First you will need to teach your dog the 'Alert Game'. This is an activity that your dog loves because it involves a lot of positive interaction. There are a few ways to teach your dog this game.

<u>Method 1</u>
Start by tying your dog's leash to a solid piece of furniture, with the leash attached to your dog's flat collar. Now you will back away from your dog and stand just barely out of reach. Take a tasty treat (something your dog will be very excited about, such as small bits of hot dog) and hold it right next to your dog's nose, then bring your hand and treat to your stomach and say 'alert'. Make sure your leg is the only thing within reach of your

dog. You are trying to encourage your dog to reach for the treat with his paw. When he reaches out with his paw he will touch your leg. As soon as your dog touches your leg give him the treat immediately and say 'good dog'. You will usually have to move the treat to your dog's nose, then to your stomach over and over in order to get him very excited about it. Be sure to move the treat slowly away from your dog's nose at first – if you move it too quickly he will get discouraged at the great distance between himself and the treat and won't try to reach for it.

After a few sessions of being tied to the furniture, your dog will learn that touching his paw to your leg is the desired behavior. Then you will want to practice without him tied.

You will want to practice this game randomly throughout the day, making sure to start him in different positions, standing, sitting, laying down, while walking, and with him on different sides of you. It is more difficult for him to paw at you when he is laying down or walking next to you, which is why you need to practice it in so many ways.

Method 2
Start by having your dog sitting in front of you, while you are sitting in a chair. Take a tasty treat (something your dog will be very excited about) and hold it right next to your dog's nose, then bring your hand and treat to your stomach and say 'alert'. You may need to wave the treat in the air above his head to entice him. You are trying to encourage him to crawl up in your lap to get the treat – but you will stop him and reward him the second his foot touches your leg on his way up. Then gently push him down and start over. Soon he will learn that you are asking him to simply touch your leg with his paw, and not to crawl into your lap.

Next you will lean against a wall with your legs slightly bent, similar to how you were positioned in the chair, but now you are more upright. Encourage him to touch your leg with his paw just as you did before, making sure to give the vocal cue 'alert' in conjunction with your hand signal.

Next move away from the wall and stand straight while giving the command. Make sure this is a fun game for your dog.

You will want to practice this game randomly throughout the day, making sure to start him in different positions, standing, sitting, laying down, while walking, and on different sides of you. It is more difficult for him to paw at you when he is laying down or walking next to you, which is why you need to practice it in so many ways.

Combining the Alert Game with your medical condition:
Once you are certain that your dog loves the Alert Game, you will stop playing it and wait about two weeks where you don't play it at all.

Once you realize you are having a panic attack, anxiety attack, flashback, etc. you will

start playing the game with your dog over and over again, until your anxiety ebbs away. Make it fun for the dog, even if you don't feel well. You may only realize that you've had an attack after the fact. Sometimes that is unpreventable, but make sure to play the Alert Game as soon as you realize you've had the episode. You may need to ask friends and family to interrupt you if they see you are showing the symptoms – that way you can play the game with your dog. This can be difficult at first – if it were easy, you wouldn't need the dog in the first place. But overtime, with your consistency, your dog will learn that you only play this amazing game that he loves when he notices the signals of your medical condition. When he senses the signals of your medical condition he will paw at your leg in anticipation of the game. When he does this reward him and give him a jackpot of treats.

In the future your dog will be interrupting your destructive behaviors so you can redirect and focus on your dog.

Problem Solving;
If your dog begins to paw at your leg whenever you are holding food you will need to correct him. Before you correct him make certain you are not feeling anxious – he may actually be alerting to your anxiety, and not just asking for the food.

<u>Deep Pressure Therapy</u>

Deep Pressure Therapy, or DPT, is a form of therapy that is very useful for your dog to perform directly after he has alerted you of your medical condition. Now you can refocus on your dog, and then allow your dog to comfort you and assist you with recovery.

With Deep Pressure Therapy you will need to sit either on the floor or on furniture. After you are already sitting you will lure your dog onto your lap by saying 'touch' and bringing your hand across your body. Start by touching the treat to your dog's nose and say his name, then lure him to your side, then move the treat over your body and say 'touch'. It is important that the dog come from your side, and not at an angle or from in front of you. If this is a large dog you will only want his front legs in your lap. Once he is in your lap make sure to give him the treat and say 'good dog'. Now you will pull your dog close against your abdomen. Having the pressure against your abdomen will assist in relieving anxiety, and it will help to give you an overall sense of calm.

Some doctors will prescribe a device called a medical wrap for various psychiatric conditions. This wrap is similar to a corset but it puts most of the pressure against the patient's abdomen to assist with anxiety relief. We are asking your dog to apply pressure in a way very similar to the medical wrap.

When your dog is in your lap be sure to pet him calmly and tell him he is a good dog. This will encourage him to stay in your lap for an extended period. Petting your dog will also help to relax you.

If your dog fidgets, squirms, is obnoxious about licking your face, or tries to get down, correct him until he relaxes. If your dog is not calm, how can you expect to be?

Once your dog is doing this command well, you will change the vocal cue from 'touch' to 'paws up'. Eventually you will be able to say 'paws up' without a signal and your dog will understand.

You can also change the command slightly by laying on your back instead of sitting up. In this case you would lure the dog directly over your abdomen, instead of over your lap.

Corner

Some handlers would benefit from a dog going around corners ahead of them. In this task the dog's body is simply creating more personal space for you as you navigate around the corner.

This task is better performed in training with the help of an assistant. There are two methods listed so you can practice alone, or with an assistant. This task requires training with the use of many corners, in many different settings. You may want to start by using the corners of walls in your home, then move into other environments.

Method 1

Give your assistant a treat and have them stand directly around a corner. Have your dog on leash and say 'corner' while pointing towards the end of the wall. Then you will pull him forward around the corner. Your assistant will give the dog the treat as soon as the dog comes around the corner. Practice this way a few times, then end the session.

In your next session you will do everything the same, except for that your assistant will tell your dog to sit, and wait until he sits before giving the treat. Practice this way for a few sessions.

In later sessions your assistant will not tell the dog to sit, but will simply wait to give the treat until after the dog sits on his own.

In this method the dog is learning that it is positive to go around corners, and if he sees someone on the other side he will not barrel them over to get a treat, but will sit politely. When you follow your dog around the corner later you will call him over to heel, and give him the treat yourself.

Method 2

If you do not have an assistant you will point towards the corner while giving the command 'corner' and lead your dog around the wall. You will have already placed a treat on the ground before the session. Show him the treat and allow him to eat it, then redirect him with the 'watch me' command and give him a treat for looking at you.

After some time you can try new corners, and toss a treat on the ground after you go around the wall. To your dog it will seem like the treat came from out of nowhere.

Eventually you will wean away from finding a treat every time, but he should still search the ground, and then look at you when you say 'watch me'.

Patrol

Some handlers are uncomfortable coming home to an empty house, with the fear that someone may be waiting inside. In this case it may be useful to train your dog to patrol the house, and to alert you if someone is inside. Again, due to liability purposes, the dog is not trained to do this to protect the handler – but the handler is still alerted if someone is in the house so they can leave for safety.

This is a task that should be practiced in your home. If you travel often, you may need to conduct training sessions in various locations. You will need various assistants for this task.

You will start by having your assistant walk inside your home and stand inside your house, against a wall. At this point they are not hiding from the dog. Make sure they have a tasty treat for your dog. Instruct them to be very quiet.

Once they are well hidden you will start at the entrance of your home with your dog. Say 'patrol' and point inside. You will then walk your dog through an exact pattern through your home, on leash. Make sure you follow this pattern in each training exercise. Your dog will become accustomed to traveling in the same pattern later, even when you are not walking by his side. As you walk with him you may stop to open closet doors, look behind curtains, etc.. Eventually you will come upon your assistant who will tell the dog to sit, and then give the treat.

After doing this a few times your assistant can then hide, perhaps inside a closet, behind curtains, under the bed, inside a bedroom, etc.. When the dog comes across them now they will not tell the dog to sit, but will wait for your dog to sit on his own, and then offer the treat.

With much repetition you will start at the entrance of your home and give the command 'patrol'. Then release your dog from his leash. By now he is excited to find your assistant with the treat. When he finds them he will sit patiently. Your patient should wait a while to give the treat, only seconds initially, but after a while should wait minutes. Your dog should be patient enough to wait there for the treat.

Now that your dog has learned to wait for the treat, instruct your assistant to only give the treat some of the time. You may have your recipient call you or text you on a cell phone as soon as the dog has found them. After your dog has waited a couple minutes for the treat, tell your assistant not to give the treat, then call your dog. When he comes to you give him the treat yourself. If you are calling your dog and he does not come, and he is still waiting patiently for the assistant to give him the treat, it may be necessary to go into the house and correct him and force him to come out with you. Once you have brought him outside you would still give him the treat, even though you have forced him to come out.

Through communication with your assistant you will change it up for your dog.

Sometimes your assistant will not be in the house at all, in which case you are waiting for the dog to come back to you to get the treat.

Sometimes your assistant will be in the house, and having the dog sit patiently in front of them. Other times you will have your assistant wait in a closet with the door shut. When they hear the dog outside the door they can slide a little treat out under the closet door, or open the door a crack to give the treat, then tell the dog to sit, and have the dog wait a while before giving another treat.

On your instruction there will be times when the assistant gives the dog a treat, and other times when you would call the dog back out to you.

In training you will want to use many different assistants. If you have guests to your house, ask them if they will help you. Changing assistants is important so your dog is learning to search for any person who may be in the house.

When your dog is done with training you can be assured of a few things. First you will know that your dog will go into the house and search along his patrol path for any person who may be inside. You will know that if he does find someone he will not act aggressively (which would usually only make the person run towards the entrance, towards you), but that your dog will sit patiently, in a friendly and calm manner, waiting to get the treat. You will know that if your dog does not come back to you within a specific time frame that he very likely has found someone. In that case you would call your dog back out, you would walk away with your dog, and call the police. However, if your dog comes back out to you quickly it is because he has not found anyone in the house, and you can rest with more assurance.

This is similar to teaching search and rescue, only you have trained your dog to do it in a specific area, and this task is designed to protect you from walking in on an intruder.

Search

This task is useful for handlers who lose certain items. The dog can be trained to search for the lost item and bring it back to you on command.

This is done easily with a dog who has a high drive to retrieve objects and enjoys various toys.

If you lose your keys:
Start with a keyring that has a small stuffed animal attached to it. Make sure your dog isn't the type to swallow the toy if it is too small. Play fetch with the toy, and each time you tell him to get it say 'find the keys'.

Praise him profusely when he brings it back to you, giving him a good scratch all along his body, followed by exchanging the toy for a treat.

In this picture you can see the keyring toy being dangled over the dogs head. You can see how excited the dog is to play with the toy.

Once he is retrieving it well tell him to do a 'down stay', toss the toy, then release him by saying 'find the keys'.

Next you will tell him to 'down stay' while you place the item across the room. Do not toss it. Then tell him 'find the keys' and allow him to go get it.

Next tell him to 'down stay' while he watches you put the toy behind a pillow on the ground. Then tell him to 'find the keys'. He will have to root around the pillow to move it. Next time you will have several pillows on the floor and let him watch you put it under one of the pillows. Then release him with 'find the keys'.

Next, take him out of the room while you hide the key ring under one of the pillows. Then you can allow him back in the room and tell him to 'find the keys'. He will know it is under one of the pillows, but now has to use his nose to find which one. Praise him ecstatically when he finds it. This game now holds a new meaning for him.

Continue by hiding the keyring in a slightly different place each time, slowly away from your original location, until he is finally searching the whole house for your keyring. The final step is to attach the keyring to your keys, and then actually losing them.

If you lose your cell phone;
Start with a padded cell phone or camera case. Play fetch with the case, and each time you tell him to get it say 'find the phone'. Do not have your cell phone in the case while you are throwing it, unless you want a broken cell phone.

Once he is retrieving it well tell him to do a 'down stay', toss the case, then release him by saying 'find the phone'. Next you will tell him to 'down stay' while you place the item across the room. Do not toss it. Then tell him 'find the phone' and allow him to go get it.

Make sure you are always rewarding him profusely when he brings it back to you. Give him a good back scratch before you take it out of his mouth. When you do take it out of his mouth exchange the case for a treat and tell him 'good dog'.

Next tell him to 'down stay' while he watches you put the case behind a pillow on the ground. Then tell him to 'find the phone'. He will have to root around the pillow to move it. Next time you will have several pillows on the floor and let him watch you put it under one of the pillows. Then release him with 'find the phone'.

Next, take him out of the room while you hide the case under one of the pillows. Then you can allow him back in the room and tell him to 'find the phone'. He will know it is

under one of the pillows, but now has to use his nose to find which one. Praise him ecstatically when he finds it. This game now holds a new meaning for him.

Continue by hiding the case in a slightly different place each time, slowly away from your original location, until he is finally searching the whole house for your case. The final step is to put your phone in the case, and then actually lose it.

Find the Car

This is something that everyone could use help with. If only we had the nose of a dog.

You will start by having your dog right outside of the car, and let him watch you put a bowl of treats right inside the door. Say 'find the car' and take any tension off the leash. You can point towards the treat if you'd like. When he moves to the car this is the only time you will let him pull on the leash. Because he is leading you to the car he will have to be walking ahead of you, and we want him to be excited to get there quickly. When he gets to the car he may try to hop in to get the treats – but don't allow him to. Tell him to sit, and then bring the bowl out to him, put it on the ground and let him eat a few bites.

You will repeat this several times, backing away from the car a few feet each time, repeating the cue of 'find the car'. After a few sessions of this close the car door so that you will have to open it once there to take the treats out. From a greater distance he may be scenting your car instead of the treats, and may even be scenting the tracks you left as you left the car so he can find it again. Regardless he will lead you back to the car for his bowl of treats.

You will need to practice this in several parking lots. In the beginning you will need to start at the car and back up. Eventually he should be able to help you find your way out of a store, through the exit, across the parking lot and to your car.

At home always tell him to 'find the car' as you are walking out. Always have treats waiting for him in the car.

Keeping You Focused

Many handlers have trouble concentrating on certain tasks. This is an example of how to train your dog to keep you focused on reading. This is useful for school reports, work projects, or even just to help you stay focused in reading for leisure.

With this task you are teaching your dog to get impatient when you stop reading aloud. Some dogs will paw at the book, nudge the book with their nose, or even stare intently into your eyes if you stop reading, which will redirect you back to the book.

Start with an old children's book that has 7 pages or less. You will sit on the same level as your dog and let him watch you put treats on each page, pushing the treats flush against the binding of each page. Then close the book.

When you open the book let your dog take the treat right out of the first page, then read a few words, and turn the page. When you have turned the page he gets to take the next treat. Read a few more words then turn to the next page, etc..

You will continue in this manner, reading a few words out loud with each page, then allowing him to take the treat on the next page. At the end of the book there is a jackpot of treats waiting.

Once your dog has learned to watch the pages for the page turn (and next treat), stop reading and don't turn the page. If your dog shows the slightest sign of distress over this pause continue reading and turn the page immediately.

You are teaching him that if you stop reading it will just take longer for him to get the treat. You will then graduate to longer books with longer phases of reading in between each page turn. Then you will start to put treats only on every other page, then every third page, etc.. Make sure that you always have a treat waiting for your dog at the end of the section you will be reading so that he does not lose interest.

Brace

Brace is a task that is usually reserved for Mobility Assistance Dogs, but in many cases psychiatric medications can have a side effect of making patients dizzy, causing lack of balance, difficulty standing from a seated position, etc..

This task will require a large breed dog. Bracing harnesses are available for purchase on many online stores, however I have found that for the purpose of assisting with dizziness that the harnesses are generally not needed.

To teach brace you will start with your dog on the left of you in the heel position. Start off by walking, then you will stop and reach over to put slight pressure on his shoulders and/or back with your hand and say 'brace'.

If he tries to sit you will immediately reach under his stomach and lift lightly up against his abdomen forcing him to stand. Make sure to say 'brace' again while doing this.

You can reward him for bracing by giving him a good scratch on his lower back. You won't want to use treats as a reward because he may think you want him to sit. This is because you likely used treats to teach him to sit earlier on.

You will want to practice this while walking, and while standing still. You will likely experience dizziness during both.

Once he has mastered this you will begin training him every time you are rising out of bed or out of a seated position. Call him over to you, then lure and adjust his body sideways along yours by using the 'touch' command. Now that he is along your side you will say 'brace' and put light pressure on his back as you stand. Make sure to reward him with the scratch.

As long as your dog is over two years old you can gradually increase the pressure you put on his back. If you have a young dog whose joints are not mature you may end up hurting your dog with time, so be careful.

Overall make certain that he enjoys helping you in this way by offering lots of praise and encouragement.

In Conclusion

Just like people, a dog is never done learning. This book has given you a foundation to build upon. Just because your dog has learned everything in this book, there is no reason for him to stop learning new things. Teach him something new.

Understanding how to communicate with your dog is the first step into a new world.

Always be conscious of how your dog views different situations. Remember he is not human and does not see the world through your eyes.

Always give him reasons to assist you through motivation and praise. And while he is your friend, you are also his leader.

Above all take care of him, and he will take care of you.